SHOWTIME FOR THE SHEEP?

THE CHURCH AND

THE PASSION OF THE CHRIST

T.A. McMAHON

CO-AUTHOR OF
THE SEDUCTION OF CHRISTIANITY

The Berean Call

BEND • OREGON

Except where otherwise indicated, all Scripture quotations in this book are taken from the King James Version of the Bible.

Italics used in Scripture references are added for emphasis by the author.

A free monthly newsletter, THE BEREAN CALL, *may be received by sending a request to the address below, or by calling 1-800-937-6638.*

To register for free e-mail updates, to access our digital archives, and to order a variety of additional resource materials online, visit us at: www.thebereancall.org

SHOWTIME FOR THE SHEEP
Copyright © 2004 by T.A. McMahon
Published by The Berean Call
PO Box 7019, Bend, OR 97708

ISBN: 1-928660-13-4
Library of Congress Control Number: 2004105903

Printed in the United States of America.

CONTENTS

INTRODUCTION

. . . .

As SOON AS Mel Gibson's directorial end-credit popped up on the black screen, I made a dash up the aisle while searching my jacket pockets for my cell phone. Hardly anyone else stirred, giving me clear sailing to the exit. I wanted to hang around to see how people were reacting to one of the most controversial and highly publicized films in decades, but there was no time. As I ran from the theater, my mind was also racing with thoughts about what I had just experienced. Moments later I was at my car talking to a Seattle TV news reporter shortly before she was to go on the air. She knew from The Berean Call's website that we had had some reservations about the film prior to seeing it, and she wanted our critical perspective after we had viewed it.

What should I say? The news program's audience would be mostly the unsaved, yet I couldn't stop thinking about believers who had seen or who would eventually see this film, many at the encouragement of their pastors. Furthermore, she told me that my input would be limited to a couple of sentences. I don't remember exactly what I said, but as I recall it went something like this: "Having spent a number of years in the movie industry, particularly as a screenwriter, I appreciated Mel Gibson's craftsmanship in bringing his personal vision of Christ's crucifixion and death to the screen. Technically, it's a superb movie. On the other hand, as one who loves and studies the Scriptures, I would not let Mel lead a Bible study in my home. His vision does not square with the Word of God."

Of course, that was just one filmgoer's rushed and somewhat emotional reaction. My drive home that evening was more of the same. My mind was still racing. Concerns I'd had previous to seeing *The Passion of the Christ* were colliding with images from the big screen itself. I was in a car wreck once, and I can still vividly remember being driven home from the emergency room: every possible thought of what, how, and why it had happened, as well as fears regarding a host of potential consequences, battled for attention in my head. Every physical activity around me seemed to be reduced to slow motion by comparison. This day was not unlike that one.

If what I related above seems to be a bit too emotional to allow objectivity about this subject, I appreciate that concern. Let's hope I can get past that initial reaction in this introduction and get on with a presentation of content that is the result of objective reasoning. Common sense may also contribute, but *biblical sense* is my goal. I hope that readers will also be aware of their own emotional biases as they come into play. That may not be easy for any of us. After all, for the most part, I'll be discussing a *movie*. Try quantifying, "I loved it!" "I hated it!!"

"It made me laugh"; "It made me cry"; "It changed my life"; "It put me to sleep"; "It's the greatest film ever made"; "It stunk!" Opposing reactions such as these toward movies of all kinds have kept spouses from talking to each other for hours, if not days. Emotions are the lifeblood of the film medium. The more a movie captures the emotions of its audience, the more effective the movie.

Tens of thousands of tickets were purchased by evangelical churches and organizations so that their members could attend Mel Gibson's theatrical production of an historical event recorded for us in Scripture—the most important of all time and eternity. The mega-churches led the way, but small churches throughout the country were not left out. They urged their congregations to support what they called a "true-to-life, biblically accurate presentation." The list of endorsers for *The Passion* seemed to lack no well-known Christian leader. Denominational lines quickly disappeared in the wake of widespread enthusiasm. A massive herding of the sheep was taking place throughout Christendom, and the flocks were being (and continue to be) driven to a *movie*. Is that a good thing?

On the other hand, there are many believers (including those who have not seen the film) who are taking advantage of the notoriety of *The Passion* to share the biblical Jesus and His gospel of salvation with anyone who wants to talk about the movie. That's a great thing!

This brief book is an attempt to sort through some of the issues critical to what is an extraordinary phenomenon in the contemporary evangelical church. Although it addresses Mel

Gibson's blockbuster film, it does so only as something significantly symptomatic of those things that are progressively taking place within the evangelical community: the trend toward the use of entertainment and amusement to teach the Word of God, the trend toward the advancement of ecumenism (specifically with Roman Catholicism), and the trend toward the subjective interpretation of the Scriptures (e.g., paraphrased Bibles and movies translated from the Bible). It is my prayer that this manuscript will offer some edifying insights that we can all take to heart, as we who know Him seek to grow in our love for our Lord and Savior, stay true to His Word and way, and fulfill the ministries to which He has called every one of us.

—*T.A. McMahon*

PROLOGUE

· ·

For I have not shunned to declare unto you
all the counsel of God.

Take heed therefore unto yourselves,
and to all the flock, over the which the Holy
Ghost hath made you overseers,
to feed the church of God, which he hath
purchased with his own blood.

ACTS 20: 27-28

SHOWTIME FOR THE SHEEP?

IN PAUL'S FIRST LETTER to the Thessalonians, he exhorts them to "prove all things; hold fast [to] that which is good" (5:21). His encouragement to the believers in Thessalonica is to make sure that their beliefs—and the resulting practices—are consistent with what the Word of God teaches. To young pastor Timothy, he writes: "Take heed unto thyself, and unto the doctrine…"(1 Timothy 4:16). Paul exhorts believers in Corinth to examine themselves to see "whether ye be in the faith" (2 Corinthians 13:5). *Personal* conviction, however, is more likely to take place than *group* conviction. Recognizing that there may be something wrong, especially when we're participating in it with our brothers and sisters in the Lord, is the exception rather than the rule.

The body of Christ, however, is not without those who would bring our attention to a problem about which we, along with others, may have been oblivious. In my years as executive director of The Berean Call, I have read thousands of letters from those who receive our ministry newsletter. Of the various groupings, my favorite by far is "the missionary-on-furlough-who-can't-believe-what's-going-on" category. Why is that? They offer terrific insights and confirmations. Most people in that category have been away from the U.S. for several years, and they have usually been in a mission field where the pace is slower and change is measured in decades rather than months or years. Upon their return to the U.S., they are quite often shocked at changes that go unnoticed by the folks living here. They write to us about their concern over changes in their churches: radical deviations in doctrines, strange ecumenical programs, startling alterations in worship and music, very different approaches to evangelization, and so forth. They clearly see the trends that have developed in their absence and confirm much of what we write about. Yet, today, some changes are taking place so quickly that one doesn't need an extended time away from America to become aware of them.

Consider this scenario. Suppose I went on a short-term mission trip in January of 2004 and returned to the United States a month or so later. When my wife picks me up at the airport, she replies to my "What's new?" query with the following information: "Right after you left, a famous Hollywood actor and Academy-Award-winning director began promoting an R-rated motion picture about the crucifixion of Jesus. The star said his film reflects his conservative Roman Catholic understanding of the four gospels, the teachings of the Council of Trent, the mystical visions of three nuns, and the liturgy of his Latin Rite Church.

He considers it a very Marian film." I interrupt with, "So? Other than the distinct Catholic emphasis, biblical films are hardly new...." Giving me a can't-believe-it-herself look, she replies, "Tighten your seatbelt. The movie may become the number-one box office hit of all time." My jaw drops. She adds, "There's more. The chief supporters of the movie are not Catholics but... evangelicals!" "No way," is all I can blurt out. "It's beyond what you can imagine," she says. "Throughout the country, evangelical churches of every size, shape, and denomination are buying hundreds of thousands of tickets and exhorting their members to pray for the film and take everyone they know to see it."

Had I actually been told such things upon returning from a short trip, I would have tried to convince myself that I had gotten caught in some kind of time warp. Sure, there has been widespread dialoguing between various evangelical denominations and the Church of Rome for years. And, yes, there has also been a growing resistance to evangelizing Catholics by most of the influential church leaders and pastors in the U.S. But nothing has developed (to my knowledge) to hasten the occurrence of such a mind-boggling event. Perhaps there's something I'm missing here.

What could possibly induce—almost overnight—evangelical shepherds all around the country to herd their flocks to feed on unabashedly Roman Catholic straw? How could this have happened? Furthermore, Catholicism is not the only critical element in all of this. Not by a long shot. Ecumenism, entertainment, and being weaned from the Scriptures all play substantial roles in the events taking place in the church today.

In the pages ahead I will address what I believe are vital issues that every believer needs to consider, especially every pastor, elder, or teacher in the body of Christ. Though I will be expressing my opinions, they are not uninformed opinions. Regarding movies and entertainment, my degrees are in the visual arts: design, film, and television. My professional experience in the movie industry spans twelve years and includes advertising, publicity, production, and screenwriting for major film studios and production companies. Regarding ecumenism and other anti-biblical trends influencing the church, I have been writing about such issues for more than twenty-five years. Regarding Roman Catholicism, I lived it for nearly three decades—most of those years as a pre-Vatican II follower of the Latin Rite Mass and the doctrines of the Council of Trent. In addition to those experiences, I hope I hold this in common with the majority of the readers of this book: a love for the truth and a desire to please the Lord in all that I do.

Showtime for the Sheep? is a question that begs a litany of other questions. But let's take the title question first. Is the church being ushered into the realm of entertainment as a means of attracting the lost and sustaining the faithful? It looks that way. But is that necessarily a bad thing? Some Christian leaders are arguing that this is the only way we can reach and teach this visual, music-oriented, TV-nurtured generation. That seems to make sense, but can it be accomplished without undermining the Word of God?

Is a dramatic production, whether a skit or a multimillion-dollar motion picture, an appropriate medium for communicating the gospel? When the Word of God is acted out, does that constitute "adding to the Scriptures?" When biblical figures are presented on screen, how close do they need to be to the original characters? What about the representation of Jesus? Can anyone play the One who said, "He that hath seen me hath seen the Father" (John 14: 9)? Is it even biblical to make such an attempt? If one is to be confident that "showtime for the sheep" is an effective and necessary way of doing church and evangelizing the lost, then he needs to face these questions and resolve them.

What of the ecumenical issue? Have the evangelical sheep been led to a movie that entertains them with "another gospel"? Are the Catholic influences, such as the emphasis on physical suffering for the expiation of one's sins, the prominence of Mary, and the mystical legends and traditions of the Church, worrisome to anyone? Apparently, these are of little concern to each of the dozens of highly influential evangelical leaders promoting the film.

Although the questions raised in this chapter (and others) will be addressed later, I need to make a crucial point here about the Roman Catholic issue. The gospel according to the Church of Rome is a false gospel. Believing it cannot save anyone. Roman Catholic dogmas such as baptismal regeneration, the Eucharist, and purgatory are a rejection of Christ's gift of salvation—paid for in full—by Him on the cross. To truly love Catholics means to share that truth with them, not to embrace a work that denies the biblical gospel. But is Mel Gibson's *Passion* truly so Catholic that it could prevent many viewers from understanding and believing the true gospel, which alone can save?

During the preparation of this book, I had numerous conversations with those who saw the film and loved it. I did little arguing with them, using the opportunity to ask questions instead. Almost every question found on these pages has been put to one or more advocates of *The Passion*. Until I talked to them, few had given much thought to the issues I raised, either prior to or right after seeing the movie. They were all hard pressed to come up with answers they themselves were comfortable with. Nevertheless, almost everyone eventually settled for something like this: "Yes, but...I know the Lord is going to use this to bring many souls into the Kingdom." If that's truly the case, we can thank the Lord for His grace and mercy. When our hearts want so much to tell the world about Jesus and the salvation He alone provides, our enthusiasm may not be tempered by discernment, nor our emotions controlled by an overriding desire to do things God's way. Moreover, it raises the age-old question: "Do the ends justify the means?"

We will be addressing whether or not pragmatism is a principle of Scripture. Those who are leaning heavily on the side of how evangelicals can use the film as a witnessing tool in spite of the negatives don't seem to be thinking of another practical concern: What harm will the negative aspects of the movie do to the sheep and the prospective sheep? If damage should occur as a result, how does one *practically* go about undoing it?

Is all the excitement for *The Passion of the Christ* a significant marker in the seduction of the evangelical church? Has it opened the floodgate for ways and means, which, though seeming to be successful for the short term, will produce "unfruitful works of darkness," rather than "the fruit of the Spirit [which] is in all goodness and righteousness and truth" (Ephesians 5: 9–11)? Those passages of Scripture in Paul's epistle to the Ephesians give God's marching orders to every disciple of Christ in these last days before our Lord's return—days the Bible characterizes as perilous and spiritually deceptive. We are to prove "what is acceptable unto the Lord. And have no fellowship with the unfruitful works of darkness, but rather reprove them."

For those who desire to exercise discernment, religious content is usually the first thing to be scrutinized. However, the medium of film presents some other issues that need to be challenged. For openers, are its methods of dramatizing and presenting the Scriptures and the gospel "acceptable unto the Lord?" Could the medium itself be at odds with what the Bible teaches? Stay tuned. ◀))

IS THE MEDIUM
THE MESSAGE?

• •

MOVIES ARE MANIPULATORS. But that's what most of us love about them. We buy our tickets, enter a darkened room, flop ourselves down in a cushioned seat, and for a couple of hours or so we may sporadically laugh, cry, gasp, jump, scream, hide our eyes, notice our heart pounding, fall in love (or, more likely, in lust), hate someone, cheer someone, want revenge, hope for reconciliation, or fall asleep. Movies can do all this to us, and more. It's an amazing process.

It's like taking a ride on a rollercoaster, except that movies are far more complex and a great deal less honest. A rollercoaster may make us laugh, scream, or cry, but nearly all of that is a response to a physical stimulus. A sharp right turn may surprise us, but there are no mind tricks involved. A roller-coaster ride is very straightforward; deception rarely plays a part. Motion pictures, on the other hand, take us on a mental ride through the manipulation of our senses and emotions. They can even make us feel that we are physically experiencing a rollercoaster jaunt, all created by camera work and sounds that emulate the real life situation we would go through at an amusement park. Although our seats never budge, the urge to fill a barf bag can become a reality.

Mastering the art of movie making involves learning to orchestrate the feelings of the audience. A good screenplay is a blueprint of "emotions," which the actors, director, cameraman, art director, costume designer, music composer, and dozens of other skilled craftsmen use to help them manage the moods of the filmgoer. Every scene is fashioned to elicit a specific emotional response. All the contributing elements—music, lighting, sound effects, and so on—are geared to that same end. It's fascinating how these do their jobs.

Take music, for example. Every film student has likely seen a demonstration of the effect that music has on a scene. A drama-less image is presented—usually a close-up of a person or wide angle of a landscape. Different types of music are then introduced. It's amazing how an idyllic forest scene can be transformed instantly into a horrifying environment (likely concealing the hounds of hell!) simply by adding a scary music score. Anyone familiar with the movie *Jaws* knows that a recurring piece of music playing over the scene of a tranquil body of water announces the unseen presence of a terrifying 20-foot-plus great white shark and is the key to getting the audience to mentally scramble for the beach.

Movies manipulate our minds. They are all about influencing the thoughts of the viewer. For nearly every successful film, credibility is a critical factor—even in animated features. People will make certain allowances, but when a film ceases to be plausible, the audience will generally abandon it. Bad acting, witless dialogue, cheap sets, poor camera work—one or all of the above can sound the death knell for a movie: "It wasn't believable!"

Although the production of a motion picture involves the creative input of scores of people, the best movies are usually shaped primarily by one individual: the director. He (or she) brings his vision to the big screen. Often he will wear additional hats such as writer and/or producer, giving him more control over the story and the production. If the story is taken from a novel or a screenplay written by someone else, the director's job is to translate the words that person has penned into images representative of what the writer had in mind. It's not an exact science—far from it. As one who has had his scripts translated into motion pictures, I know it never ends up being the movie one originally envisioned. That can be a great disappointment, although, on occasion, through the collaborative process involving wonderful artists, the story can be translated into a production that greatly exceeds the original vision of the writer. It may not end up being what he had intended, but its success has a way of salving wounded pride.

Casting a film is an important part of the manipulative process. Beyond the necessary ability to act, an actor's physical appearances are often significant in sustaining the credibility of a film. A fifty-year-old superstar won't cut it as a high school student; an established comedienne might have problems as a believable Mother Teresa; diminutive Danny De Vito shouldn't be cast as the lead in the life story of André the Giant. If the audience isn't convinced that an actor is credible in a part, the so-called movie magic can dissipate rapidly. Again, once a film ceases to be believable, it will inevitably lose the interest of its viewers.

All of the things mentioned above contribute to the creative process of movie making. By their very nature, films, in order to be successful, must manipulate the emotions. Does that make the medium *inherently* evil? No. No more so than a good storyteller who shapes his conversation in order to set us up for a great punch line. Although today my list of recommended movies might fit on the head of a pin, there have been films over the years that I consider worthwhile. Even so, we need to be aware of how a motion picture's influential nature can be used for evil. The Nazi propaganda films viewed by German audiences in the 1930s and '40s are classic examples of brainwashing devices that promoted racial superiority while instilling hatred for Blacks, Jews, and other non-Aryan peoples. Also, given the immoral content of most films today, I can understand and empathize with those who shun movies just as they would avoid a plague. An acquaintance claimed that the only thing that might induce him to go back to a theater would be to see biblical stories on the big screen. He was hardly convinced by his own words, and I am even *less* convinced regarding biblical stories.

As was noted earlier, sharing one's views about movies can be comparable to walking through a minefield of emotional reactions. That's understandable because, as I have demonstrated, feelings are the main stuff of cinema. If there is no emotional reaction to a film, there is almost nothing to talk about, or probably nothing *worth* talking about. However, when a movie has a powerful emotional effect on the viewer, it may be difficult at best to discuss it objectively. Yet, it is possible to nudge the discussion toward a more objective arena. In an attempt to do just that in order to make a case against using the film medium to present biblical content, I turn to basic math. Let's add together some of the particulars of movie making, with both the presentation of the content of the Bible and the way Holy Scripture itself prescribes communicating its content, and see how it tallies.

A movie begins with a script, which itself may be an adaptation of a novel. The screenwriter tries to understand and translate the words and thoughts of the novelist, and the film director attempts to do the same with the final script. Both processes involve major changes that are highly subjective. Once shooting is under way, the vision becomes that of the film's director. Does the same thing happen when one attempts to translate the Scriptures to the screen? Yes. However, we may not recognize that as a problem until we remember who wrote the source material. Is a man entitled to change or adapt God's written Word? No. Will God's Word suffer in translation? Yes. Can a director's visual rendering on the screen truly reflect the God-breathed Scriptures? Does it improve Scripture or make it more easily understood to dramatize it?

What about historic accuracy? Is the Bible historically accurate? Absolutely. If that were not so, it could not truly be God's Word. That Scripture is one hundred percent accurate in all that it records is an irrefutable fact. Should a visual representation of situations that are revealed in the Bible also be accurate? Some might argue that movies are art and not historical records. I don't know what that means, beyond admitting that a movie is, of course, inaccurate. Though artists have for millennia drawn from the Scriptures for their subject matter and have created many aesthetically pleasing works, where have any of these provided true spiritual enrichment? It's not possible. Why? At best, they are human misrepresentations that appeal to the flesh. Yet God's Word condemns such distortions and makes it crystal clear that "the flesh profiteth nothing" (John 6:63).

The cinema is mostly about visuals. Usually the medium is most effective when dialogue is kept to a minimum. This is one reason that, in direct contrast to the Bible, which is God's objective Word, a movie is a very *subjective* form of communication. For example, the saying, "a picture is worth a thousand words," is rarely true, because a picture does not invite specific or direct responses. A yes or no to seeing a beautiful sunset would be odd indeed. Normally, such a picture evokes endless lines of poetry brimming with emotionally charged words. Although the Bible is not without descriptive language, it is purposefully limited in that regard and never depends upon that to carry its message. This presents an insurmountable problem when it comes to translating the content of the Bible to the screen—unless, of course, one doesn't have a problem with filling in the visual blanks and describing scenes beyond what the Word declares, even though adding to Scripture is prohibited according to Revelation 22:18 and other verses.

Orchestrating the elements in order to manipulate the emotions of the audience, as we've seen, is what movies do. How does that square with the way the Bible goes about communicating its truth? It doesn't. The Word of God never appeals to one's emotions, nor does it persuade people on the basis of feelings. Though its truth may have an effect on our emotions, that consequence is always a *by-product* and never the *means* for spiritually transforming our lives. How, then, could a movie that is attempting to communicate the subject matter of Scripture employ a method, i.e., the manipulation of emotions, that is contrary to God's Word? That's more than a little inconsistent. Moreover, a movie has no other options *beyond* manipulation, because it can do nothing else and succeed.

Reviewing the "math" in all of this, I hope you can see that the tally thus far is not favorable to movies as a medium for communicating biblical truths. Notice also that nothing presented in this chapter has been specifically directed at *The Passion of the Christ*. It applies to all films that either aspire or pretend to translate the Bible. I have no doubt that many who are involved in projects that translate Scripture to the screen are sincere in their efforts, just as are most who produce paraphrased "Bibles." Yet the irony is that their efforts are actually drawing people *away* from the Word of God. Could both endeavors be related and, in fact, be a major contributor to the evangelical church amusing itself away from the Scriptures? That question will be considered next. ◀꒰

AMUSING OURSELVES AWAY FROM THE WORD?

● ●

WHEN WE HEAR THE WORD "amusing," we usually think of it as referring to something humorous or related to having fun. A particular form of entertainment may even come to mind. However, the word has other definitions that many of us may not have considered. "Amuse" also means to *divert* or *delude*. Amusement is certainly a diversion, particularly from the serious things of life. When we break the word down, we gain some interesting insights. Musing, for example, means to "consider thoughtfully or at length." Psalm 143:5 gives us that understanding: "I remember the days of old; I meditate on all thy works; I *muse* on the work of thy hands." Yet, adding the prefix "a" (denoting "unconcerned with") to "musing," produces the adjective *a–musing*, defined as "unconcerned with giving thoughtful consideration."

In view of the voracious appetite for entertainment in the world today, it wouldn't be out of line to suggest that serious thinking may be on the wane. That's not a social commentary but merely an observation. It's rather obvious that there are multitudes among us who "just wanna have fun!" The idea of "having fun" may even seem natural to some, but it's a latter-day perception. My reprint of Noah Webster's 1828 *American Dictionary of the English Language* gives this definition of the word "fun": "Sport; vulgar merriment. *A low word*" (italics in original). If we didn't know that definition was common nearly 200 years ago, we might think it was recently reformulated to describe the activities of Super Bowl 2004 with Janet Jackson and cast! Of course, that's not to deny that good, clean fun exists, or that it has a worthwhile place in our lives. Nevertheless, we need to recognize it for what it is and how it is influencing our lives.

When entertainment, or amusement, takes the reins in attempting to teach us about matters of serious consequence, the outcome will be a delusion. Some may find standup comedy during brain surgery amusing in a TV sitcom, but few would be comfortable knowing that such a "fun" element was a required course for their doctor's medical degree. Clowning around, combined with performing life or death medical procedures, rarely produces good results. The same can be said for issues of a spiritual nature that affect our temporal life and eternal destiny. Entertainment has its place, but there are some places where it is out of bounds.

The Bible is not a light-hearted, fun-loving book. Though its content produces inexpressible *joy* for the serious reader, its clearly stated purpose is God's revelation to mankind, in His own words: "Man shall not live by bread alone, but by *every word* that proceedeth out of the mouth of God" (Matthew 4:4). Through the Scriptures, the Holy Spirit reveals what man can't figure out on his own about God, and about himself: the depths of man's depravity, God's overwhelming love for humanity, His solution for man's sin problem (which demonstrates His love), and the eternal consequences for those who either accept or reject His solution. Such things are of a serious and vital nature.

This does not mean that the Book cannot produce responses that are joyfully uplifting. The Old Testament, erroneously characterized by some as nothing but wrathful, is filled with wonderful expressions of joy by God's people in reaction to God's words. "Thy testimonies also are my *delight*," wrote the psalmist (Psalm 119:24). The Queen of Sheba recognized the fruit of God's wisdom given through Solomon's teaching: "*Happy* are thy men, *happy* are these thy servants, which stand continually before thee, and that hear thy wisdom" (1 Kings 10:8). The Scriptures describe the Israelites as "*glad* and *merry* in heart for the goodness that the LORD had shewed unto David, and to Solomon, and to Israel his people" (2 Chronicles 7:10). The New Testament, as well, is rife with upbeat emotions experienced by believers as they grow in their relationship with our Lord through the reading of His Word. Peter writes regarding the appearing of Jesus Christ: "Whom having not seen, ye love; in whom, though now ye see him not, yet believing, ye rejoice with *joy unspeakable* and full of glory" (1 Peter 1:8).

Although there are numerous other kinds of reactions (grief, confidence, sadness, dread, conviction, guilt, hope, comfort, fear, etc.) that accompany the reading of the Scriptures, such emotions are a *by-product* of God's truth. Never does the Word contrive emotional situations to persuade its readers.

Amusement, fun, and entertainment are concepts that are incompatible with the Bible. Such words denote a process that is inconsistent with an activity that requires one's thoughtful or earnest attention. They are all about *diversions* from serious thought. When applied to biblical content, such diversions by their very nature undermine the way God would have us approach His Word. This is serious stuff.

The psalmist writes, "Blessed are they that keep his testimonies, and that seek him with the whole heart" (Psalm 119: 2). Peter declares that we are "born again...by the word of God" (1 Peter 1:23). Jesus tells us that we are to be sanctified, or set apart, by God's Word: "Sanctify them through thy truth: thy word is truth" (John 17:17). David gives us no "amusements" in referring to the law, statutes, commandments, judgments, and the testimony (i.e., all the Scriptures) in Psalm 19:

> The law of the LORD is perfect, converting the soul:
> the testimony of the LORD is sure, making wise the
> simple. The statutes of the LORD are right, rejoicing
> the heart: the commandment of the LORD is pure,
> enlightening the eyes. The fear of the LORD is clean,
> enduring forever: the judgments of the LORD are true
> and righteous altogether. More to be desired are they
> than gold, yea, than much fine gold: sweeter also
> than honey and the honeycomb. Moreover by them
> is thy servant warned: and in keeping them there is
> great reward. (Psalm 19:7–11)

Paul admonishes us to be diligent in our study and handling of the Scriptures so that we might understand and communicate that which is "approved unto God" (2 Timothy 2: 15). Again, this is serious business. When amusement, fun, and entertainment enter into handling the Word of God, no matter how sincere the attempt, the *trivialization* of the Word takes place. Moreover, an old-fashioned meaning of the word *amuse* applies: to *deceive*. Paul was concerned about such issues in the fulfillment of ministry when he wrote: "But [we] have renounced the hidden things of dishonesty, not walking in craftiness, nor handling the word of God deceitfully; but by manifestation of the truth commending ourselves to every man's conscience in the sight of God" (2 Corinthians 4:2).

Please note that the concern here is not about using amusement, fun, and entertainment to draw the lost to hear the Word of God. That approach can sometimes have its uses but, sadly, it can also encourage hosts of outlandish abuses. Nevertheless, that is not our subject. The issue before us is incorporating "entertainment" into the communication of scriptural truth.

It would be very easy to fill the rest of this book, and many more volumes, with what most would consider extreme examples of attempting to teach the Bible through amusement. Here are a few advertisements: "*The Beverly Hillbillies Bible Study* is a church-growth tool that also helps with the perpetual problem of recruiting outstanding Sunday-school teachers." This company also offers "*The Mayberry Bible Study*, with Andy, Barney, Opie, and all your old friends" and "*The Bonanza Bible Study*," with Hoss and Little Joe. Featured as well is "*The*

DVD Bible Study, starring the *Dick Van Dyke Show.*" A recent article from *Charisma Online News Service* featured a church in Tennessee that has patterned their mid-week service after David Letterman's late night TV program, complete with a "Top Ten" list with a religious tone. The pastor acts as the "host," beginning with a monologue and backed by a live band. The program is broken up by musical interludes.

What about animated vegetables that talk about God? To date, more than 25 million copies of *Veggie Tales* videos have been sold. The latest episode currently in production is titled *Sumo of the Opera.* Its promotional blurb states: "The plot is hush-hush for the moment, but it's been described as *"Rocky* meets *Mikado* meets professional wrestling—with a biblical lesson to boot." This is not just amusement for the kindergarten set!

My guess is that I just lost a number of readers. If you are on the brink of joining their ranks, take a deep breath and consider the term *trivial.* Is it possible that a talking cucumber, albeit a clever and witty one, may be trivializing the Word as it attempts to deliver "a biblical lesson"? One dictionary sums up the meaning of "trivial" by saying that it "refers principally to things that have little importance or significance in themselves or that require no intellectual depth on the part of persons concerned with them." Not that that's the intent of either those who create such teaching tools or those who use them. Nevertheless, that is what inevitably results by the very application of amusement-oriented products. Not only is the scenario of fruits and vegetables that preach at odds with the verses quoted above, but the method is deceitful, which the Apostle Paul cited as an issue of concern in 2 Corinthians 4:2. Why have *Veggie Tales* sold 25 million-plus videos? Is it because of the biblical truths they may contain? Or is it because they are cute and funny and entertaining? Obviously, entertainment is the overriding element. That concept has to be maintained for the videos to continue to be successful, yet they will certainly draw upon biblical content—that is, those things not so serious or sacred that they can't accommodate entertainment. But what part of God's Word might that be? Remember, this is not the same as a *Road Runner* cartoon, which has no aspirations beyond pure amusement. *Veggie Tales* has attracted millions of Christians on the basis of its "biblical" content, yet has sold them a message that, at best, has trivialized that content.

Although it has no talking tomato, the animated motion picture *Prince of Egypt* would seem to be another rather obvious example of dumbing down a biblical event. Scarcely anyone would object if such stories were fiction or ancient myths. But that's not the case. Throughout history, great efforts were taken by copyists to make sure that *every jot and tittle in every line* of the Bible was meticulously recorded. That's imperative with a Book that declares that every word in it is "given by inspiration of God." How great a gap is there, then, from painstakingly produced copies of the Bible to a two-hour animated film about Moses, who was a type of Christ? "But," someone might complain, "you can't compare cartoons with the Word. No one takes them seriously!" Tell that to the producing company that had evangelical scholars help with the movie's biblical content and accuracy in order to win (which it did, in droves) an evangelical audience.

What does the translation of the Scriptures into the animated cartoon medium do to the message? If the medium is just meant to amuse and no one takes it seriously, could that be a proper vehicle for God's truth? What, then, of an attempt at making a cartoon biblically accurate? That's a problem also, because accuracy is an absurdity in an animated cartoon. I hope it's becoming evident that, even though many animated productions are created for the purpose of sincerely edifying people through biblical themes, they will inevitably trivialize the serious content and wind up amusing their audiences away from the Word.

Unlike animated films, dramatic productions are often astounding in their realistic presentation of historical events. It would seem, then, that they are better suited to present the content of the Bible. But "better suited" is a relative comparison. Is "better suited" the standard we want to use in our evaluation of the conversion process of biblical events into a dramatic motion picture? Can the medium do it justice, or will something significant be lost—or added to—in the translation process? ◄))

LOST IN TRANSLATION?

• •

SOME THINGS don't translate well. A novel, for example, that mostly conveys the thoughts parading through the minds of its central figures would be difficult to translate into a medium that features visual imagery. Although the stream of consciousness from a main character may be both stimulating and thought provoking, if it has to be communicated through narration, it will lose that which makes films most effective: dramatic visuals. Image is everything in the movies. Some novels are great for the screen, while others would make better radio programs. Even those films that have overcome the translation difficulties and have turned out to be box office successes are not without their detractors. The chorus of "hated the movie, loved the book" will always haunt films taken from popular novels.

Although personal criticisms of movies are usually opinions relating to likes and dislikes, some assessments have a more objective basis. For example, a person who says he loved the book more than the movie might note that the film was able to cover only a small portion of the book. He might complain that his favorite scenes from the book never made it onto the screen. The same might be said about the book's characters: a few may have been left out, and a new one who seemed to combine more than one role may have been added. Finally, and most subjectively, there's the protest that the images presented on the screen were not the way the critic imagined them when reading the novel.

The common response to those who mount a "hated the movie, loved the book" criticism is that a movie cannot legitimately be compared to a book because the two media are distinctly different, and each must therefore be considered only on the basis of its own characteristics. Some ardent fans of Mel Gibson's *The Passion of the Christ* are offering that line of reasoning to those who complain that his film subverts the Bible. Mel himself has said that his film is *not* a documentary on the Bible and should not be viewed that way. He likens it to a work of art. Shouldn't that satisfy those who want to nitpick over his visual interpretation of what is written in the Scriptures? It depends on how one views the Bible, and more importantly, how true that view is to what the Bible itself teaches.

To begin with, translating content from the Bible to the screen is in some ways similar to translating a novel, but in one extremely important way there is no comparison: God is the author of the Scriptures. His Book is absolutely unique. It was written over a period of 1,600 years by 40 men living in different cultures and having various occupations. Yet it reads throughout as though it were the work of one mind, which it is—that of the Holy Spirit (2 Timothy 3:16). The apostle Peter explains that God's Word did not come "by the will of man: but holy men of God spoke as they were moved by the Holy Spirit" (2 Peter 1: 21). Phrases such as "Thus saith the Lord" and "The word of the Lord came to me" are found more than 4,000 times throughout the Bible.

The proof that the Bible is just what it claims to be is confirmed by 1) its historical accuracy, attested to by archaeology, 2) its accuracy in matters related to science, confirmed by *true, empirical science*, and 3) prophecy—the foretelling of events hundreds and, in some cases, thousands of years prior to the event taking place. The transformed lives of millions of souls who have read and believed it is also compelling evidence for the supernatural origin of the Bible. Prophecy, however, is its irrefutable proof. One-fourth of the Scriptures are prophetic, and they are not shrouded in ambiguities.

As just one example, specific details regarding the crucifixion of Jesus were described by David in Psalm 22 and by the prophet Isaiah in chapter 53 of the book referred to by his name. The particulars foretold who would be at the scene, how they would react, what the Roman soldiers would do to Jesus, the very words He would utter, that no bones of His body would be broken, that He would be pierced, that He would be buried in a rich man's grave, and numerous other precise details—yet these prophets of God lived 1,000 and 750 years respectively before the birth of Christ! Furthermore, at the time of both writings, stoning, not crucifixion, was the practice among the Jews for putting lawbreak-ers to death. Crucifixion would not become a common means of public execution until adopted by the Persians (c. 500 B.C.), fol-lowed by the Greeks and the Romans centuries later.

The criteria the Bible places on itself as to whether or not it is truly God's Word is what one would expect from something God authors: perfection. If it is found to be inaccurate in what it claims, or false in what it predicts, we are to junk it! Not, however, because that would mean it was just another religious book conjured up by men, but because it would be a *fraud*. As we noted in the last chapter, the Bible takes itself very seriously: "It is written, that man shall not live by bread alone, but by *every word* of God" (Luke 4:4).

One would think that the very serious nature of the Scriptures would send any God-fearing man running from the task of translating it. Yet aren't there a host of Bible transla-tions—everything from the fiercely defended King James Version to the self-serving New World Translation of the Jehovah's Witnesses? The goal of every honest translation team is to produce the most accurate translation possible, based on the most reliable Greek and Hebrew manuscripts available. Although there are no original manuscripts in exis-tence, thanks to God's grace in preserving His Word we have a Bible that, in every way, *is* the Word of God. While that has been attested to in volumes of scholarly books and is not the subject of this one, consider this rather simple piece of sup-porting evidence. Based on the Dead Sea Scrolls, dated around 140 B.C., we know that the Old Testament we read today is accurate. There is no doubt that, years later, Jesus read those *same scriptures* and leveled no recorded criticisms of them in the New Testament. Regarding the New Testament, there is more evidence for its accuracy related to the originals than there is for any book of antiquity.

Problems, however, can and do arise. They occur primarily when men deviate from the objective to the subjective, i.e., when they go from the science of accurately translating the Hebrew and Greek languages to following their *feelings* in regard to what the text says—and, ultimately, what it means. Although some translations lean toward subjectivity, that error is pervasive among the many popular *paraphrases* used today. Unlike translations, which are a collaborative effort by a panel of scholars with expertise in the original languages (the New World Translation translators excepted), paraphrases are usually the product of one man's "vision." Eugene Peterson's widely used *The Message* is a prime example of how extraordinarily subjective a paraphrase can become and still have the audacity to be promoted as God's Word. What are the consequences? They are comparable to a sailor making intuitive adjustments to a true compass. At first, the errors may not be noticeable, but the longer one sails, the farther from the course he strays. Deviating from what God *said* to what someone *feels* He said is delusion heading for spiritual disaster.

If diverging from a literal translation of the Word of God to a paraphrase introduces serious error, what about attempting a *visual* translation? Although a paraphrase stays within the boundary of the medium of words, there seem to be no confines for deciding what a word means beyond the interpreter's personal biases. For example, in *The Message* (Msg), Peterson puts a humanistic spin on Philippians 4:7 ("And the peace of God, which passeth all understanding, shall keep your hearts and minds through Christ Jesus" –KJV). By contrast, he writes, "Before you know it, a sense of God's wholeness, everything coming together for good, will come and settle you down" (Msg). How does he interpret John 1:14 ("And the Word was made flesh, and dwelt among us…" – KJV)? "The Word became flesh and blood, and moved into the neighborhood" (Msg). The only guideline in this sort of interpretation is what the "translator" *imagines* would better communicate the notion of a scripture verse. If the subjectivity of a paraphrase cuts us loose from the objective moorings of God's words, what will a textual-to-visual image translation do?

Mel Gibson and his "visual paraphrase," *The Passion of the Christ*, should compel every believer, whether he or she has seen the film or has no plans to see it, to consider the "word-to-visual image" question and arrive at an answer consistent with what one believes the Bible teaches. Why? The film itself will influence both believers and non-believers for years and will foster the abandonment of any reservations the evangelical church has had about using visual images for the communication of biblical themes. Facing the issues involved should help us to rethink our acceptance of a host of other productions, from the cute to the evangelistic to the profane—from *Veggie Tales* to the *Jesus* film to *Judas* and the hordes of other religious films that will follow in the wake of *The Passion*'s success.

Was Mr. Gibson aware of the task before him? By that, I'm not referring to those matters pertinent to launching a multi-million-dollar film production. He has been there, done that, and received the movie industry's highest honors for doing it well. The task I'm referring to is translating a book written by God to the big screen! There's no doubt that he was aware of the sensitivities of different religious groups, but did he have any idea of what he was undertaking from a biblical stand-point? In bringing to the screen the final hours of Christ before and including His death, he needed to translate the words of Scripture into images.

One major hurdle among many others he faced was that the Bible is not a screenplay. Not even close. It offers very little in the way of description, and movies are the stuff of descriptions realized. Where there were gaps deliberately left by the Holy Spirit, Mel and his collaborators filled in as they saw the need, for the sake of art and dramatic continuity. In addition to creating scene after scene based upon what is—and what isn't—in the Scriptures, he had to cast the characters presented in the gospels. A screenplay usually gives vivid descriptions of its main characters. The Word of God does not. We're told, for example, what the disciples said and what they did. Period. However, that's not good enough for the medium of film; more visual substance must be added. But should God's Word be sub-jected to such "enhancements"?

Peter has to look and act like a take-charge character who would be believable lopping off the ear of a servant yet, at the same time, able to convey guilt and sorrow when he rejects Jesus. The lines he says and the way he says them must conform to the subjective vision of the director. All of the same applies—for the movie's sake—to the other biblical figures whose presence is required for the screen story, i.e., the story in the mind of the director.

The process, as you can see thus far, is at odds with biblical truth. If the only way to make a quality film about the Bible—that is, one with all of the ingredients necessary for a *successful production*—is to manufacture ideas out of one's imagination, isn't that corrupting biblical truth with extra-biblical content? "But a movie is not the Bible," someone might argue. True. But what if it is accepted widely as a *visual translation* of an event presented in the Gospels? When a movie such as *The Passion* is perceived as portraying biblical content in the most accurate way it can, and when evangelical leaders across the country attest to its biblical accuracy, should not the film be scrutinized the same way one would scrutinize a television evangelist or anyone else feeding us religious content? Shouldn't we search the Scriptures to see if "it is as it was"? ◀🔊

IS IT AS IT WAS?

• •

A SMALL ITEM of controversy that hovered over *The Passion of the Christ* was the supposed comment of Pope John Paul II after viewing the movie. It is alleged that he said, "It is as it was!" Although that's a terrific line for the promotion of the movie (thereby inciting skeptics), there is solid evidence that he indeed made that statement. Why didn't he simply confirm what he said? Speculation has it that it was denied by those close to the Pope for two reasons: 1) Given the objections to the film by many Jewish leaders, they might take offense at his taking a favorable view of the film; 2) Mel Gibson's anti-Vatican II beliefs as a Tridentine Catholic might cause the Pope some embarrassment. To that, I would add a third point as to why the Pope's cohorts should have wanted to withdraw his comment: Because it's rather silly! How could he know that "It is as it was" unless he was there?

The advertising and publicity team for the movie may have been put off by the confusion surrounding such a great ad line, but they regrouped and turned to the dozens of evangelical leaders and scholars testifying to *The Passion*'s historical and biblical accuracy. To these people we must raise the same question: "Were you there?"

For the sake of argument, and to demonstrate the absurdity of the declaration that the movie is historically accurate, let's just say that somehow those making the claim *were* there. They could, therefore, compare what they saw on the screen with their "historical experience." Not good enough. They would only be recognizing what others had brought to the screen as historically true. Those others, that is, every creative contributor to *The Passion* production, would also have had to be there and somehow managed to have accurately reproduced whatever had been supplied for the film. The costuming for ancient period films, for example, may be convincing but is no more than an educated guess. I certainly wasn't around at the time of Christ, yet the costume worn by *The Passion*'s Mary character seemed more reminiscent of a nun's habit I remember from my parochial school days than what may have been first-century garb. At the very least, for lack of information, I think we can dispense with the historical accuracy delusion.

So, what about the biblical accuracy of *The Passion of the Christ?* Many New Testament scholars, including evangelical seminary professors, have answered in the affirmative. That's more than curious. It makes you wonder if in their test for accuracy these religious academics grade on a curve. How many biblical inaccuracies disqualify *The Passion* from being officially rated as biblically accurate? Does the film lose points for including extra-biblical items?

The movie opens in a garden scene, where the Jesus character is praying. So far, so good? Not really. Although the Bible tells us that Jesus prayed in the Garden of Gethsemane, the film supplied far more information than that given in the Scriptures. Moreover, the location selected to film the scene is *not* the Garden of Gethsemane. The site was selected and then enhanced, no doubt, by the director to *convince* the audience that what they are seeing *is* the Garden in which Jesus prayed. If that sounds deceitful, it is—but not with malicious intent. That's just what movies do. It's part of movie magic. By the way, when I use the words "movie magic," I'm simply referring to all the ingredients of the film medium that work together to captivate, or draw, an audience into the drama unfolding on the screen before them.

The question that needs to be resolved, however, is: Does movie magic mix with biblical truth? The answer applies not only to *The Passion* but also to every endeavor at translating the written Word of God into visual media. Will something be lost in the translation, and if so, how serious a matter is it? Even the most conscientious attempt by the most Bible-conscious filmmaker at reproducing a biblical scene (even at the exact location!) would be the product of movie magic. "Accuracy" is not the most important issue to a filmmaker. If the actual Garden, for example, doesn't look the way the director envisioned, or if he thinks the audience may not "buy it," he will look elsewhere. He knows he must find a place that is *believable* on the screen.

When respected evangelical leaders who had screened *The Passion* prior to its opening (and encouraged multitudes of believers to attend) stated that the movie was true to the Scriptures, what they were actually saying (without being aware of it) was that Mel Gibson's vision of what took place during the last 12 hours in the life of Christ was *believable*. Some were so *convinced* that, at the time of this writing, they had seen the movie more than a half-dozen times! As hard as that may be to fathom, I don't know of any of the enthusiastic shepherds— especially those who preach and teach the Scriptures—who gave a warning to the sheep concerning the obviously extra-bib- lical material in the film. To do so could have sent a "negative" message to the flock, thereby dampening the general enthusiasm for the movie.

Were the pastoral promoters so mesmerized by movie magic that they missed, in the opening garden scene, the serpent's tail dangling from a hooded figure's nostril before it slithered over to the Jesus character, who then rose up from prayer to crush its head? Is that simply symbolism for Satan's defeat, as some have argued? Perhaps, but it's *Mel's symbolism*—achieved by taking liberties with God's Word, in addition to borrowing from a mystic's vision (see chapter 7).

Those evangelicals who sang the praises of the film's "cre- ative license" shared no concern that the Bible declares that an *angel* came to Jesus in the Garden of Gethsemane to strengthen Him, *not* the devil to tempt him. Biblical "accuracy" lost its meaning at the outset of *The Passion* and never recovered it throughtout the rest of the movie.

The scene with the serpent in the (wrong!) garden was followed by one with "Jesus" being knocked off a bridge, where he dangled momentarily from chains as he traded looks with Judas. These things occurred in the first fifteen minutes of the film, and one would think that by that time many of those who expected the movie to be biblically true would have headed for the exits.

Instead, they were treated to much more of the same: Mary is awakened with the intuitive knowledge that her son is in danger, Mary Magdalene tries to have the Roman soldiers stop the interrogation of the Jesus character by the Jewish leaders, and two of the Jewish leaders attempt to defend "Jesus" and are removed from the interrogation hall; "Jesus" flashes back to a time when he crafted a table and had a playful exchange with his mother. These and the following are from notes I took at my initial screening. I include only those that I thought most viewers might catch:

Peter denies "Jesus" without a cock crowing; as he calls Mary "Mother," Peter kneels before her, acknowledging his guilt over denying her son; Mary crawls along the floor of the Praetorium until she senses her son in a dungeon beneath her; Judas is harassed by demons posing as children, or vice versa; Herod exclaims that "Jesus" is "not guilty of a crime—he's just crazy"; Satan arrives at the scourging of "Jesus" with a midget demon in tow; Pilate's wife gives Mary linens; Mary and Mary Magdalene mop up the blood of "Jesus" in the scourging arena with the linens; "Jesus" carries his cross and falls repeatedly; Mary is involved in a silent face-off with Satan; Mary goes to "Jesus" as he falls under the weight of the cross; a flashback shows Mary running to "Jesus" as a young child;

"Jesus" quotes a verse from the Book of Revelation to his mother; a Roman soldier is awestruck by Mary; a Catholic saint (Veronica) is featured with her daughter; Veronica captures the blood-stained imprint of the face of "Jesus" on her veil; Simon of Cyrene has numerous extra-biblical lines of dialogue; the garment of "Jesus" is ripped apart; "Jesus" cries out as he is nailed to the cross; the cross with "Jesus" upon it seems to levitate before it is placed in the ground; as the cross is put in place, Mary alone among the followers of "Jesus" is standing; Mary kisses the blood-drenched foot of "Jesus"; Satan floats through the crowd at Golgotha; a sponge of sour wine is presented to "Jesus" on the tip of a spear; for rejecting "Jesus," one of the thieves on the cross has his eye plucked out by a raven; a tear drop from God above seems to cause an earthquake that splits the Temple; blood and water from the pierced side of "Jesus" spray a Roman soldier, causing a "spiritual transformation"; Satan is shown in a desolate abode, seemingly bound there; the body of "Jesus" is partially draped across Mary, recreating Michelangelo's *Pietà*.

At what point in *The Passion* could we say that the words "biblical accuracy" and "scriptural integrity" cease to be applicable? What could those who love the Word of God possibly be thinking as the above images parade past their eyes and fill their minds? My guess is they *weren't* thinking—at least not biblically. They were "experiencing" movie magic. "Not so," says the evangelical who's seen *The Passion* a couple of times, "I see it as art!" Interesting. I know a little about art, having earned a bachelor's degree in fine arts. Nevertheless, I'm puzzled by what the person means who says, "I see it as art."

There must be a thousand definitions of art—most of them related to the idea that an art form must be aesthetically pleasing. It's usually a visual thing but doesn't preclude the other senses. *The Passion of the Christ* certainly qualifies by that "hardly official" definition. Mel Gibson himself stated that he created it as a work of art. However, we can't be sure that his response was not simply an attempt to fend off the objections to his having included so many extra-biblical scenes and concepts in his movie. You see, he also said that he wanted to be true to the Gospels and that he believed he was helped by God to produce *The Passion.*

Can an evangelical enthusiast for *The Passion* get away with crying "art" in the face of objections to its taking numerous and outlandish liberties with the Gospels? Certainly, but in so doing, all he is saying is that *The Passion* is an aesthetically pleasing production that perverts the truth of God's Word through the interpretive vision of Mel Gibson and his fellow craftsmen.

One highly visible evangelical leader, who couldn't praise the movie enough during a TV interview, kept repeating that every Christian needed to "experience" it. That sounds like a good thing, but what exactly is the audience of *The Passion* experiencing? Perhaps Mel can tell us.

EXPERIENCING MEL'S VISION

• •

MAKE NO MISTAKE about *The Passion of the Christ*. It *is* Mel Gibson's vision. In the foreword to the book that features the photographic images taken during the production of the movie, he writes,

> People often ask me why I wanted to make a film about the Passion of Our Lord. My usual response is that I've wanted to make this film for over ten years, which is true. That seems to answer the question for most.
>
> The reality, of course, is more complex and had its genesis during a time in which I found myself trapped with feelings of terrible, isolated emptiness. Because I was brought up to be a good Christian and a good Catholic, the only effective resource for me was prayer. I asked God for his help.[1]

I have admiration for the man. After reading scores of interviews and articles, some tremendously candid on his part, that admiration hardly wavered. I've never met him, except in a vicarious and genetic sort of way: my oldest son took a university class titled "The Films of Mel Gibson," and Mel showed up to provide his personal insights.

My admiration, however, goes deeper than my son finding him likeable (though it's a definite plus). We have a few things in common. We were both raised in devout Roman Catholic homes—"devout" simply meaning that our families took our Catholic faith seriously. He is a Tridentine Catholic. He chooses to worship according to the canons and decrees of the Council of Trent (a.k.a. Tridentine Council, taken from the city of Trent's ancient name, *Tridentum*). Trent was an "infallible" Church council convened primarily to address what Rome considered to be the heresies of the Reformation.

In the 1960s, the Church convened the Second Vatican Council. "Vatican II," as it is commonly called, re-established and emphasized Trent's dogmas (*Lumen Gentium*, VII, 51), yet introduced significant changes. One such alteration affected the liturgy of the Mass. Prior to Vatican II, the Mass was conducted only in Latin; since then, the liturgy is recited in the language common to the people wherever the Mass is said. Tridentine Catholics reject many of the reforms of Vatican II and believe that only a Mass said in Latin is efficacious. They believe that *transubstantiation*, a ritual process in which the priest is said to turn bread and wine into the "body and blood, soul and divinity" of Jesus Christ while the elements remain "under the appearance of bread and wine," takes place *only* in the Latin Mass.

I ceased attending Mass in the mid-1960s, so my only remembrance of the Mass is in Latin. As an altar boy, the language (which I learned by rote, having almost no understanding of it) seemed magical to me. Some priests that I served would sing out the words with such authority that I knew heaven *had* to respond to their incantation. I didn't realize that Protestants had their own views on the subject, so I was shocked to learn that they mocked the Latin words *"hoc est corpus"* (used in transubstantiating the bread into Christ's body) by corrupting them into "hocus pocus," denoting a hoax or fraud.

It's interesting that Mel chose Latin and Aramaic for the dialogue in his film, a rather risky choice, because it could turn off an audience; yet, he knew something. He told the director of a Catholic TV network,

> I go to the old Tridentine Rite. That's the way that I first saw [the Mass] when I was a kid. So I think that that informs one's understanding of how to transcend language. Now, initially, I didn't understand the Latin. But I understood the meaning and the message and what [the priests] were doing. I understood it very fully and it was very moving and emotional and efficacious, if I may say so. There is a lot of power in dead languages.[2]

But he's also keenly aware that the real power of movies is in *imagery*, which is heightened when dialogue fades into the background.

I don't agree with Mel's theology, but I can't take anything away from his film know-how, abilities, and especially his nerve. When I first heard he was going to do a religious movie in the ancient languages with no subtitles, I laughed—long. I didn't need my own experiences working for major studios and production companies over the years to recognize a disaster in the offing. Knowing about Mel's Catholic background, I could only think at the time, *He'd be better off running the gauntlet in purgatory than trying to get that film off the ground in Tinsel Town!* I knew that no priest he ever knew could give him a comparable penance. Sure, he's Mel Gibson, superstar! Mel Gibson, Academy Award-winning director! Even with those credentials, saddled with a project like that, all he would be able to get would be as many meetings with studio execs as he wanted, and the door shown to him after each one. Upon exiting, he would probably hear them laughing as he went all the way down the elevator and out to his car.

He would get no dough, no distribution, and no deal from anyone. In addition, he broke the cardinal rule—the only rule in a business with no rules: Never Invest Any of Your Own Money in Your Film! But he was on a mission. He put nearly $30 million of his own money into the project. That was either saintly or suicidal.

I admire Mel. He believes he was on a mission from God. I don't. He flew the mission like a *kamikaze* (thunder of the gods!) and not only did he complete it against overwhelming odds, but he kept the faith of his vision and has been reaping its financial rewards beyond his wildest expectations. If financial success is the gauge of God's involvement, there's no argument. But that's never been the measure for spiritual truth. Jesus said that abiding in His Word is the criterion for knowing truth (John 8:31,32). Let's therefore consider Mel's vision in that light.

First of all, it's *his* vision and he's fierce about it: "I don't know if I will ever work [in Hollywood] again. I've said that this is a career killer and it could well be, but that doesn't matter because I don't care."[3] Film critic and conservative Jew Michael Medved writes, "Gibson financed the film on his own precisely due to his determination to realize his own traditionalist Catholic vision of the Gospel story without compromise to the sensitivities of profit-oriented accountants or other religious perspectives. Jewish leaders feel wounded that he never consulted them on the script or historic details, but he also left out Protestant and Eastern Orthodox traditions."[4]

As Medved recognizes, the movie is Mel Gibson's *Catholic* vision. His scholarly resources were Jesuit priests. "It reflects my beliefs—I've never done that before," Gibson told a reporter from EWTN News.[5] As noted, his Catholicism is extremely conservative. "Believe me," he confided to Peter Boyer of *The New Yorker* regarding the rigors of traditional worship, "every other brand of everything is easier than what I do." One such "rigor" is the necessity of abstaining from eating meat on Fridays. To intentionally break that rule results in the commission of a mortal sin, which condemns to hell should one die without having the sin absolved by a priest. Vatican II changed the regulation, making it voluntary throughout the year except on Ash Wednesday and on every Friday during Lent. Mel keeps it year-round!

Although there are other issues where Mel has differences with mainstream Roman Catholicism, on the dogmas (which the "infallible" Church cannot change) he and Rome are following the same catechism. The following are examples of some of the basic rigors to which every Roman Catholic is subjected: Entrance to the Church is only through the Sacrament of Baptism, which places one in the state of *sanctifying grace*, also known as being "justified." Unless one is in that state at the time of death, a Catholic can enter neither purgatory nor heaven, making hell his final abode. Continuing in sanctifying grace is essential. Receiving the Sacraments is said to maintain the process. When mortal sins are committed, the person sinning loses justification. To become justified again, one must confess his sins to a priest and be absolved. Once absolution takes place, *penance* must be performed—usually consisting of prayers such as the recitation of the rosary.

In Catholicism, salvation is a *process* involving many justifications, condemnations, and re-justifications. Most important is to be found in a *state of grace* at death—and no one, not even the Pope, can presume that he will be in that condition just prior to his death. Therefore, all Catholics must strive to remain in the state of sanctifying grace, which is accomplished through participation in the Sacraments and by faithfully adhering to the many laws of the Church. These include the required attendance at Mass on Sundays and Holy Days of Obligation, and the adding of more graces through works of devotion, penance, and charity.

There are two categories of sin in Roman Catholicism: mortal and venial. The punishment for the former is eternal—the latter, temporal. Christ is said to have paid the eternal punishment; but the sinner absolved of mortal sins through Confession, although forgiven, must pay his own temporal punishment, either here on earth or in purgatory. The *Catechism of the Catholic Church* explains (par. 1459), "Raised up from sin, the sinner must still recover his full spiritual health by doing something more to make amends for the sin: he must 'make satisfaction for,' or 'expiate,' his sins. This satisfaction is called 'penance.'"

Penances can also be performed and offered to God for others, particularly the souls said to be suffering in the purifying flames of purgatory. St. Thomas Aquinas, one of the Doctors of the Church, taught that the least pain in purgatory is far greater than any corresponding suffering on earth. St. Cyril of Alexandria also believed that it would be better to suffer every penitential torment here on earth until judgment day rather than to suffer for them for one day in purgatory. Historically (and to this day), Catholics have taken such teachings seriously.

Throughout the world, multitudes of Catholics suffer extreme forms of self-inflicted punishments such as whipping themselves, wearing hair shirts to irritate the skin, walking for miles with stones in their shoes, or crawling on bloodied knees to cathedrals or shrines to Mary. In my youth, I learned to hold in the highest regard those Saints who suffered the most. And, of course, if they were known to exhibit the *stigmata*, (having bleeding wounds similar to those of Christ, as supposedly did St. Francis of Assisi, St. Catherine of Siena, and numerous others), you'd better believe I possessed their devotional cards! This is what my former Church taught. Again, from the *Catechism of the Catholic Church* (par. 1473), "While patiently bearing sufferings and trials of all kinds and, when the day comes, serenely facing death, the Christian must strive to accept this temporal punishment of sin as grace."

Suffering for sins is a major pillar of Roman Catholicism, whether the focus is on Christ's physical sufferings or on one's own. That and all the Church teachings presented above are foundational to Mel's faith, the "rigorous" faith of his youth, to which he returned in earnest a dozen years ago. Thus began Mel's spiritual journey that set the foundation for his vision for this movie. Many evangelical Christians, however, enamored with *The Passion,* passionately want Mel to "be one of them," that is, to know the Lord in the way they do. Some evangelical leaders who have had personal contact with Mel assert that he is indeed a "believer." If true, that would be wonderful! But in order for that to be true, Mel would have to have walked *away* from the faith of his youth—not *returned* to it. The canons and decrees of the Council of Trent, which he, a Tridentine Catholic, knows better than most Catholics (and which every Catholic must obey lest they be condemned to hell), makes a clear distinction between what evangelicals understand as the gospel of salvation and what the Church teaches. Canon XXX states:

> If any one says that after the reception of the grace
> of justification the guilt is so remitted and the debt of
> eternal punishment so blotted out to every repentant
> sinner, that no debt of temporal punishment remains
> to be discharged either in this world or in purgatory
> before the gates of heaven can be opened, let him be
> anathema.[6]

The term "anathema," particularly in the context of Trent, denotes condemnation or excommunication, i.e., eternal separation from God. The "infallible" Church Council lists more than 100 anathemas, most of which address evangelical beliefs. Canon XII identifies what every truly born-again Christian believes: "If any one saith, that justifying faith is nothing else but confidence [faith or trust] in the divine mercy which remits sins for Christ's sake, or, that this confidence [faith] alone is that whereby we are justified; let him be anathema." If Mel believes everything between the "If" and the "let," he is indeed saved. However, that would also mean that he is anathematized, or condemned, by the Roman Catholic Church. On the other hand, if he does *not* believe that he is justified by faith alone, he is condemned by the Scriptures. The apostle Paul, in Galatians 1:9, spells it out for everyone (Catholics and non-Catholics alike) who would add works to faith: "As we have said before, so say I now again, If any man preach any other gospel unto you than that ye have received [Ephesians 2:8–10 and many other verses], let him be accursed [anathema]." We all hope and pray for Mel's salvation, but it comes down to what he ultimately and truly believes. He can't have it both ways.

Whether or not Mel Gibson is now saved, only he and the Lord truly know. Nevertheless, what he has brought to the screen is rooted in his Roman Catholic faith. He writes in the foreword to the photography book cited earlier, "Holy Scripture and *accepted visions* of The Passion were the only possible texts I could draw from to fashion a dramatic film" (emphasis added). We shall consider the things that contributed to Mel's vision of *The Passion of the Christ* in the pages ahead. ◄»

THE VISION MIX

• •

THE VISION FOR *The Passion of the Christ* was not something that was conjured up overnight. Mel Gibson said that it was twelve years in development, beginning with his own soul searching and a return to the beliefs of his youth. The focus of his meditation is the twelve hours encompassing Christ's suffering and death, from the arrest of Jesus in the Garden of Gethsemane to His removal from the cross. According to ABC's Diane Sawyer, who interviewed him on *Primetime*, they are "12 hours Gibson says are the beating heart of his Catholic faith." I would concur. The most serious devotional I can remember regarding the faith of my youth was meditating on the Fourteen Stations of the Cross.

In reading many of Mel's interviews, it is clear that his Catholic faith was the basis for what he brought to the screen, but it also became apparent that his faith set no strict guidelines for either the content or the approach that he would take to his project. Often when a Catholic writes a book on matters related to his faith, he will seek the approval of authorities representing the Church, who "sign off" on the book with an *Imprimatur* and *Nihil Obstat.* This is simply an official recognition that, although there are all sorts of things in the book, it contains nothing that is *contrary* to dogmatic Church teaching and practice. Mel, of course, did not look for official approval for his film; the point here is that Mel's vision is not as restricted as one might think.

There is another aspect of the Catholic Church that expands Mel's horizons. Unlike evangelicals, who accept the Bible as their *only authoritative* source for matters of faith and doctrine, Catholics look to Sacred Scriptures *and* Sacred Tradition. Vatican II explains, "...the Church does not draw her certainty about all revealed truths from the holy Scriptures alone. Hence, both Scripture and Tradition must be accepted and honored with equal feelings of devotion and reverence."[7] Tradition is a rather complex and amorphous doctrine that has to do with examining the life experiences of the Catholic faithful throughout the ages in helping to decide what is to become official Church dogma. For example, most of the dogmatic teachings related to Mary—which every Catholic is *obligated* to believe or be in jeopardy of committing a mortal sin—have *no biblical* support. The doctrines regarding Mary herself being immaculately conceived (revealed by an apparition) and her assumption into heaven—without biblical or early Church Father's support—became official teachings simply because the bishops desired them to be, and the faithful have believed it and have built shrines to Mary for generations. Church Tradition enlarges the arena for Mel far beyond what is restricted by the Scriptures.

As noted in the last chapter, Mel indicated, "Holy Scripture and accepted visions of The Passion were the only possible texts I could draw from to fashion a dramatic film." "Holy Scripture" is self-evident, but what does he mean by "accepted visions"? Accepted by whom? By his Church. There have been many visions reported by numerous Catholic mystics in Church history. Not all are "acceptable," but many are. Thirteenth-century Saint Simon Stock, for example, supposedly had a vision of Mary, Our Lady of Mt. Carmel. She instructed him to craft a brown scapular for the Catholic faithful, which, when worn with integrity and in devotion to her, would reduce one's time in purgatory. Stock's vision was approved; John Paul II, Mel Gibson, and millions of other Catholics wear a brown scapular today. There are many less spectacular visions that carry no official *Imprimaturs*, yet they are acceptable because they do not *contradict* Church dogma.

During his years of meditation on the sufferings of Christ, Mel Gibson came across material from three Catholic nuns, all mystics: Anne Catherine Emmerich, Mary of Agreda, and St. Bridget of Sweden. Emmerich (1774–1824) was a German nun allegedly gifted with amazing abilities: ecstatic levitation, visitation to different places in her spirit (including purgatory), guidance by angels, the psychic discovery of Mary's house in Ephesus, and reception of apparitions of John the Baptist and the mother of Jesus. In addition, it was said that she lived solely on the

Eucharist wafer and water for the last dozen years of her life. Her biographer reported that her suffering was extreme. Besides being continually ill, she manifested the stigmata in her hands, feet, and side and also exhibited puncture wounds reminiscent of a "crown of thorns." Supposedly, her wounds bled more on Fridays than any other day. Though we can only speculate as to the veracity of such claims, we can apply the prophet Isaiah's test to her writings: "To the law and the testimony: if they speak not according to [God's] word, it is because there is no light in them" (Isaiah 8:20).

Her book, *The Dolorous Passion of Our Lord Jesus Christ* (covered by a *Nihil Obstat* and an *Imprimatur*), is what got Mel's attention. The book claims that Jesus took her in the spirit to record historical events, including His passion. Impressed with the details she described, Mel selectively added them to fill out his own vision. Seemingly in full approval, *Christianity Today (CT)* quotes from Emmerich's book:

> [A]fter the flagellation, I saw Claudia Procles, the wife of Pilate, send some large pieces of linen to the Mother of God. I know not whether she thought that Jesus would be set free, and that his Mother would then require linen to dress his wounds, or whether this compassionate lady was aware of the use which would be made of her present.... I soon after saw Mary and Magdalen approach the pillar where Jesus had been scourged...they knelt down on the ground near the pillar, and wiped up the sacred blood with the linen which Claudia had sent.[8]

CT comments that "Gibson does not follow *Dolorous Passion* slavishly" and commends the scene for its "sympathy and compassion between the two women." There's not even a hint from *CT* that there might be a problem with such extra-biblical fiction or that referring to Mary as the "Mother of God" just might be blasphemy. Calling the mystic Emmerich's addition to the Garden of Gethsemane scene "dramatically powerful, but much more significant theologically," *CT* attempts to validate the nun's delusion, or deception: "Satan, writes Emmerich, addressed Jesus 'in words such as these': 'Takest thou even this sin upon thyself? Art thou willing to bear its penalty? Art thou prepared to satisfy for all these sins?'" *CT* here has borrowed that "theologically significant" mode of discernment from the methodology used by Rome to establish Catholic dogmas such as the Assumption of Mary: *"Potuit, decuit, ergo fecit,"* i.e., "If it could have happened, it should have happened, therefore it did happen." The magazine then describes what Mel does with Emmerich's "vision":

> Gibson shows Jesus being tempted by a pale, hooded female figure, who whispers to him just such words, suggesting that bearing the sins of the world is too much for Jesus, that he should turn back. And from under the tempter's robe there slithers a snake. In a moment of metaphorical violence drawn straight from Genesis 3:15, Jesus crushes the serpent's head beneath his sandaled heel.[9]

Why doesn't *Christianity Today* gather the many articles of a like nature to this one that it produces month after month and put them under a new department titled "Extreme Bible

Makeover"? If I seem more than annoyed at this, I am. As a former Catholic, I can understand Mel Gibson's attraction to such material, but as an evangelical —I'm appalled at *CT*'s sellout of the Bible! (More on this later.)

Mel told Peter Boyer of *The New Yorker* that Emmerich's book had some "amazing images. She supplied me with stuff I never would have thought of." The scene of a chained "Jesus" being thrown off the bridge was one "amazing image" from Emmerich. She writes, "when they were half over the bridge they gave full vent to their brutal inclinations, and struck Jesus with such violence that they threw him off the bridge into the water...."[10]

She also "saw" Judas: "Next I cast a glance outside the town, and, near the south gate, I beheld the traitor, Judas Iscariot, wandering about, alone, and a prey to the tortures of his guilty conscience; he feared even his own shadow, and was followed by many devils, who endeavored to turn his feelings of remorse into black despair."[11] Mel takes some license with Sister Anne's "spiritually guided" supplementation of Sacred Scriptures by using a gang of vicious boys to represent the demons.

Other "inspired" scenes that Mel borrowed from Emmerich and modified for the screen include Peter weeping on his knees before Mary and calling her "Mother"; "Jesus" being incarcerated beneath the Praetorium (where Mary "intuitively" locates him); the effeminate Herod, who calls Jesus "crazy"; much of the scourging scene, including the Romans turning his body to whip his chest; the crying out of "Jesus" due to the pain he suffered; details of the many falls of Jesus related to the Stations of the Cross; the torturous stretching of "Jesus'" arms to match up with the holes in the cross for his palms; and the "fountain" of blood sprayed on the soldier who pierced "Jesus" with his spear, and that soldier's "spiritual transformation."

He also used a few ideas from Mary of Agreda (1602–1665), a discalced (barefoot) Franciscan nun whose family (mother, father, and two brothers) joined religious orders at the same time. Her book, *The Mystical City of God*, supposedly contains special revelations from God. She claims that angels attended to her continuously, and, in one chapter of her book, she gives an account of Mary's time in her mother's womb from the moment after she was "immaculately" conceived. Her most famous prophecy is, "It was revealed to me that through the intercession of the Mother of God, *all heresies* will disappear" (emphasis added). No comment. She wrote that "prophecy" when she "saw" the cross to which Jesus had just been nailed flipped over. Then in answer to the prayers of Mary pleading with God that the face of her son not be smashed into the ground, unseen angels intervened, causing the cross to levitate.[12] St. Bridget, a 14th century nun, allegedly also had visions of the Passion, with details such as the Roman soldiers stretching the arm of "Jesus" nearly out of its socket to fit the cross's predrilled nail holes, and "Jesus" wearing the crown of thorns as he hung from the cross.

What I hope is becoming apparent is Mel Gibson's Catholic view of the Bible. Yes, he believes the Bible is Sacred Scripture. But, Sacred Scripture, his Church tells him, is equal in stature with Tradition. In addition, visions of the Saints and near-Saints can be very helpful to one's understanding of the Bible. That's especially useful to Mel the filmmaker, because the Scriptures provide few details. And Mel obviously doesn't take seriously the admonitions the Bible gives about reinventing the content of God's Word: "Ye shall not add unto the word which I command you, neither shall ye diminish ought from it..." (Deuteronomy 4: 2); "Add thou not unto his words, lest he reprove thee, and thou be found a liar" (Proverbs 30:6).

On the other hand, perhaps an appeal to *reason* might give some food for thought. If Scripture is sacred, dare anyone add details where it is silent? If Tradition is sacred, are movie production decisions subverting the Church's authority? If Mel believes mystic Anne Catherine Emmerich's "details" are from God, as she claims, how can he improve upon them? If he thinks she made up most of it as she went along, what's the point in using any of it? Well, for a filmmaker, the crux of the matter is not *truth*—it is creating *convincing* scenes that result in *emotionally moving experiences* for an audience.

That being the case, a major hurdle for the producer/ director of *The Passion of the Christ* was to cast a *believable* Jesus. He found someone who was the same age as Jesus Christ when He died and who had the initials J.C.

Is that a good start? ◄🔊

THE MAN WHO
WOULD BE JESUS

• •

MEL GIBSON gave a rather extensive interview on the largest religious media network in the world, Eternal World Television Network, a conservative Catholic organization founded by Mother Angelica. The host, Raymond Arroyo, was intrigued by how Mel went about selecting James Caviezel to play the role of Jesus Christ. Mel began by describing his personal image of Jesus: "[I saw Him] as a man born at that time…into that culture, and as a real workman."[13] Arroyo pressed him about the "divinity" aspect, noting that most of the previous screen "Christs" had a noticeable effeminate quality about them, perhaps intended to imply divinity. Mel had no interest in going that route. He replied, "[Caviezel's] a very masculine kind of guy, but there is something 'otherworldly' about him…that seems to envelop him like a glow. And that very presence was a key thing in casting [him].

He emits that kind of light…but that's just natural to Jim—that's who he is."[14] In another interview Mel stated, "The key to making *The Passion* was finding an actor capable of embodying to the highest degree possible both the humanity and spiritual transcendence of Jesus Christ."[15] Gibson believed he had the right man, but he put the ball in Jim's court, asking him if he knew what he was getting into.

"I told him I have to do this," Caviezel said. "We're all called to carry our cross, and if we don't carry it, we'll be crushed under it."[16] His response to Mel implied that he understood the spiritual nature of the project.

My first exposure to Caviezel was through an email forwarded to my home from an evangelical friend. It was an impersonal "*The Passion of the Christ* Urgent Prayer Request" that looked as if it had originated at a ministry, yet had made its way around the country, thanks to concerned believers. The writer identified himself as someone who had "discipled" Jim Caviezel when Jim was a student athlete at the University of Washington. He said that Jim had communicated to him that the film he was doing for Mel Gibson was "under attack" and needed prayer. The writer noted that "There are strong *non-Christian* movements which have arisen in recent days that are *extremely hostile to the Gospel*" (emphasis added). The writer said the project was undergoing "intense spiritual warfare" and closed with, "Jim is calling upon the Body of Christ to help thwart the attack of the enemy. Please be fervent in this prayer on behalf of Jim."[17] I know I read the email rather quickly, but my first thought was that Jim was an evangelical. That was a reasonable assumption, because *discipling* takes place *after* a person is saved. Months later, I began reading news stories about James Caviezel that were puzzling.

For instance, after meeting with the Pope in Rome subsequent to the release of *The Passion*, Caviezel was interviewed by the media. The *National Catholic Reporter* ended my confusion about Jim being an evangelical:

> Caviezel is a staunch Catholic who places strong emphasis on loyalty to the Church and to the pope. He said that when someone now asks if he's Catholic, he responds, "I'm Roman Catholic." As distinct from what? "From being American Catholic," he said. He is also strikingly pious. During filming, Caviezel carried relics of St. Francis of Assisi, St. Padre Pio, St. Anthony of Padua, St. Genesius (the patron saint of actors) and Anne Catherine Emmerich [as did Mel]. He also carried a piece of wood believed to be from the True Cross. Caviezel had a special compartment sown into his loincloth for the relics. He also prayed the rosary, went to confession, and attended daily Mass. "I always wanted to have the Eucharist in my body, because I felt more like I was playing Christ," he said.[18]

I was uncertain about Jim's true faith initially, because in some early articles he referred to himself as a Christian rather than Catholic, and he was saying things that seemed consistent with what an evangelical might say. That can be confusing, now that more and more Catholics are using "evangelical language." For example, a Catholic may claim to be "born-again," as I have heard quite often. It took me a while, but I finally learned to ask *when* the person had been born-again. The response is usually, "When I was baptized as an infant." I've also had Catholics tell me that they are "saved by grace." When I ask them to explain what they mean by that, their reply centers around the idea that God provides the grace to do the work toward meriting one's salvation. It's a "grace" *process*. As you can see, Catholics define these terms related to salvation in a way that contradicts what the Bible clearly teaches.

Although I'm convinced from the Scriptures that Jim believes in "another gospel" (Galatians 1:7), which is not the *true* gospel, and that I do need to pray for his salvation, I can't help admiring him (as I do Mel) for his fierce commitment to what he believes. I'm seeing little of that among professing evangelicals today. Even the liberal *National Catholic Reporter* seems to respect Caviezel's steadfastness:

> He won't be deviated for the sake of political correctness. This holds true even in conversation with the legendary Protestant minister Billy Graham. Caviezel said [Graham] once told him they should emphasize what they have in common. Caviezel's response? "Let's not go down that road. The problem is this: we water down our faiths to accommodate each other. That's what we do now in order to get along. But when we water down the faith, we accommodate each other, but we also accommodate sin. We're not supposed to say 'militancy' these days. But we're either church militant or church mediocrity."[19]

Catholics believe that their Church has a spiritual richness and depth not understood by "their separated Protestant brethren," and, as seen above, Caviezel is into every "spiritual richness" that his Church has to offer. Sadly, though Dr. Graham wanted to emphasize what Catholics and evangelicals have in common (the deity of Christ, His virgin birth, etc.), he seemed to be uninformed of the critical fact that the Church of Rome has a false gospel (explained in chapters ten and eleven) that can save no one.

Caviezel commented that when people watch the movie and see him upon the cross, he hopes it won't be Jim Caviezel they see, but Jesus Christ. That notion may shock some evangelicals, but it will scarcely faze a Catholic. An evangelical is comfortable with the idea that when a person looks at a Christian, he is "seeing Christ" because of the Christ-like qualities that he is reflecting. The Apostle Paul in Romans indicates that believers are to be "conformed to the image of [God's] Son" (8:29), and he also writes in Galatians 4:19, "My little children, of whom I travail in birth again until Christ be formed in you...." It all has to do with the *moral* attributes of Christ and nothing to do with His *physical* qualities. Catholics, on the other hand, have no problem with the physical aspects. I grew up with images of the "physical Jesus." Every cross that I can remember had a Jesus hanging on it. Every holy card featuring a cross had "Jesus" hanging on it. An empty cross was a "Protestant thing." We Catholics were more closely in touch with Jesus because we had a thousand years or more of His images, or so many of us thought. It never dawned on me, even in the art history classes I took in college, that the "Jesuses" portrayed by every artist all looked dissimilar.

As I look back on it, it makes little sense. What's the point? Since the great artists of the past were no doubt extremely thoughtful in deciding whom they would select to paint as Jesus, I suppose they, in their selections, were trying to convey those qualities about Jesus that were meaningful to them. So, although we can appreciate their aesthetic skills, what does their art do for us spiritually? Nothing—or *worse*. We have thousands of images of Jesus, all different, that personally mean something to their artists, but to the rest of us, one is no better than another—and *none* is accurate.

Yet what about that one image that sticks in a person's mind as visually appealing in its apparent likeness to Christ as one imagines Him? That's the problem. That *feeling* reflects an emotional appeal to the imagination of the viewer. Yet no matter how appealing, it's a misrepresentation that leads a person away from the *true* characteristics of our Lord and Savior. But can't the Holy Spirit still use such art to encourage people in the Lord? That's a fair question, which we'll get to a bit later.

As we search the Scriptures, almost nothing is descriptive of the physical aspects of Jesus. Isaiah 53:2 might come closest, but is hardly detailed, and there are differences in how the verse should be interpreted: "He hath no form nor comeliness; and when we shall see him, there is no beauty that we should desire him." Though some understand this to mean that Jesus may have been very plain looking, Matthew Henry, in his *Commentary on the Bible*, interprets the verse in a more figurative sense, having to do with the "low opinion that men had of him." He takes into consideration Christ's lowly conditions of birth, His hometown

("Can there any good thing come out of Nazareth?"–John 1:46),
His associations with the common people, and so forth:

> Being generally apt to judge of persons and things
> by the sight of the eye, and according to outward
> appearance, they saw no beauty in him, the beauty
> of holiness and the beauty of goodness, enough
> to render him *the desire of all nations;* but the
> far greater part of those among whom he lived,
> and conversed, saw none of this beauty, for it was
> spiritually discerned. Carnal hearts see no excellency
> in the Lord Jesus, nothing that should induce them to
> desire acquaintance with him or interest in him.[20]

Certainly David, who was a type of Christ, was a man of
physical beauty ("of a beautiful countenance, and goodly to look
[at]" –1 Samuel 16:12), and reason would tell us that Christ,
being a perfect man (without physical imperfections), would
greatly exceed David's "beautiful countenance." No one knows
for sure. But one thing *is* sure—the Bible gives *no* physical
details from which an artist might draw. In Revelation 1 and 19,
we find these descriptions of "the Son of man" who is "called
Faithful and True" (as a Catholic, I don't remember seeing holy
cards of Him fitting John's descriptions): "His head and his hairs
were white like wool, as white as snow; and his eyes were as a
flame of fire; And his feet like unto fine brass, as if they burned
in a furnace...And out of his mouth goeth a sharp sword....
And on his vesture and on his thigh a name written, KING OF
KINGS, AND LORD OF LORDS" (Revelation 1:14; 2:16,18;
19:15, 16). That's the way the beloved of Jesus—the apostle

who was so intimate with Him that he rested upon His breast (John 13:25)—saw Him. Obviously, the language is symbolic, as the Holy Spirit intended.

There is therefore literally nothing to draw from in the Scriptures for anyone attempting to visually represent Jesus. Clearly, the absence of physical description was not an oversight on the part of the Holy Spirit because when Scripture was written, "people [then] weren't as image-oriented as we are today." We can only conclude that the Lord did not intend for us to cherish *any* visual form of Christ. Paul declares, "Yea, though we have known Christ after the flesh, yet now henceforth know we him no more" (2 Corinthians 5:16). We can only conclude that all images of Christ, whether honored by Catholics or Protestants, are images of "another Jesus." ◀

IMAGES OF ANOTHER JESUS?

• •

NOT TOO LONG AGO, the *National Catholic Reporter* ran a contest asking artists from around the world to submit slides of their works that best portrayed "Jesus for the third millennium." More than 1,000 entries from 19 countries were received. The winner, titled "Jesus of the People," featured a dark-skinned, effeminate character in dreadlocks, complete with a yin-yang symbol and Indian feathers. Although it had its enthusiasts, most were not pleased. One critic wrote, "It is nothing but a politically correct modern blasphemous statement reflecting the artist's and the so-called judge's spiritual depravity." Another, commenting on the "universality" of the winning image, felt he could do better: "My Jesus will be a narcoleptic vegetarian astronaut clown mime who lives in a Sri Lankan tree with three lesbian popes and sings the boogie-woogie in Navajo. And I'll probably win." This latter critic's sarcasm highlights the utter absurdity in all of this, while the former critic describes the blasphemous nature of such an endeavor.

First, the absurdity. Whether it's a contemporary image with dreadlocks, or Salvador Dali's "Christ" represented in his *Crucifixion,* or Tintoretto's 16th century *Christ Before Pilate*, they all have one important thing in common: they *aren't* Jesus! None of them are even *close* to what Jesus looks like—not that "close" counts for anything. A picture that isn't actually of me, but *resembles* me, is still not me.

I hope it's become apparent how inane it is to have an image that is someone's *guess* as to what Jesus looks like. Yet it seems that many evangelicals don't get it. In reactions to discussions that Dave Hunt and I have had on our radio program, *Search the Scriptures Daily*, as well as personal discussions we've had with people regarding images of Christ, the great majority either thought we were being unrealistic about it (even legalistic!), or they saw it as a non-issue. The common response was, "Hey, competing images of 'Jesus' have been around so long and are so pervasive in the church that the idea of physical portraits of 'Jesus,' none of which is accurate, isn't worth getting worked up over." Is that a reasonable response? I know evangelicals who go ballistic over the absurdity of renderings in natural history museums of "prehistoric" near-humans or "creative" reconstructions of animals based on a tooth, yet who don't think twice when their Lord and Savior is subjected to the same thing.

But what does the Bible say? In Exodus 20:4 God prohibits the making of "any graven image, or any likeness of any thing that is in heaven above, or that is in the earth beneath, or that is in the water under the earth: Thou shalt not bow down thyself to them, nor serve them: for I the Lord thy God am a jealous God." This Second Commandment is an injunction against idolatry (which, curiously, was not part of the Ten Commandments that I learned at my various Catholic schools; the Second was dropped and the Tenth split into two parts). Since that law was given at the time (possibly the *exact* time) that the Israelites fashioned the golden calf, we have a straightforward example of the idolatry God was forbidding.

Today's common response in light of the commandment is, "We don't worship our images of Jesus. They are just reminders of who He is and what He's done for us." Let's wrestle with that. We've established that any image of Jesus can only be a *false* image. How, then, does a false image of Christ remind us of *Him*? Since we do worship Christ, can we filter out the false image of Him? If we have the false image of Christ in our minds when we are worshiping Him, aren't we at least verging upon idolatry? "No," someone might protest, "I don't have the false image of Christ in mind when I worship Him." So the false image is a selective-memory thing. It reminds a person of "who He is and what He's done for us," but not during worship. Many people are not given to such mind/imagery control. Some say they can't worship *without* some image in their head.

We have had reports from missionaries in India and New Guinea who are concerned about the popular *Jesus* film. They tell us that after the film has been shown to the native villagers, whose lives have been occupied with idols, they simply add the image of Jesus on the cross to the other representations of their gods. Ironically, we think we are very different from such primi-tive peoples. I remember hearing of a youth pastor who declared that the only way to reach this sophisticated, visually oriented generation with the gospel would be to "go visual." However, there are reasons why nearly all pagan idolatry is visual, and it would be prudent to investigate why that is before throwing cau-tion to the wind and launching a media blitz on this generation.

The Second Commandment is not just about the *shaping* of false gods; it also has to do with jealousy: "...for I the Lord thy God am a jealous God (Deuteronomy 5:9)." He states His love for His children Israel: "Yea, I have loved thee with an ever-lasting love: therefore with lovingkindness have I drawn thee" (Jeremiah 31:3). Yet His children turned to false images: "They provoked him to jealousy with strange gods.... They have moved me to jealousy with that which is not God...and moved him to jealousy with their graven images" (Deuteronomy 32:21; Psalm 78:58). He does not want His people giving their affections to anything that would draw them away from Him. To get a rough sense of this, suppose my wife were to pick up my wallet and find a picture of model Cindy Crawford in the photo section, tucked in between the pictures of our children. With a hurt expression on her face, she asks me for an explanation. I reply that the beauti-ful model reminds me of her. Even if she recognizes that I am quite sincere, that does not completely erase her hurt feelings or the jealousy generated by the fact that someone—who was not she—was given a place in my "those-who-are-near-and-dear-to-me" photo collection. For the sake of our relationship, the truly loving thing to do would be to dump Cindy.

IMAGES OF ANOTHER JESUS?

In the New Testament Book of Acts we find, "For as much then as we are the offspring of God, we ought not to think that the Godhead is like unto gold, or silver, or stone, graven by art and man's device" (Acts 17:29). We are being instructed here that humans are the creation of God, but idols are the creation of humans. Other Bible versions translate "man's device" as his thoughts or imagination. The clear meaning is that any attempt by man to fashion ideas about God, whether through his art, his devices, or his imagination, is idolatry. No matter how good they make a person *feel*, they are *lies*. When man's ideas are fashioned into images of Jesus, the result is a false Jesus—"another Jesus"—not the one preached by Paul under the inspiration of the Holy Spirit (2 Corinthians 11:4).

There is little doubt in my mind that Mel Gibson sincerely and honestly wanted to present a Jesus to the world whom he honors in his heart and sees in his imagination. The problem is that none of this is good enough. He or anyone else "sincerely and honestly" attempting to do the same will end up with "another Jesus." I was working at 20th Century Fox Film Corporation in publicity and advertising when a film came along that was somewhat different from our normal fare. It was titled *Gospel Road* and was promoted as a "musical anthology of the story of Jesus." The film was shot on location in Israel, and Johnny Cash produced, scored, co-wrote, and sang songs throughout. One particular publicity photo for the movie became an item of surprise and humor in our department. It was the photo of the actor who played "Christ." Everyone was convinced that *I* posed for the shot! This was in my before-coming-to-know-the-Lord days.

My hair was down to my shoulders and I had a full beard. I took the publicity "still" home to show my mother "my photo." She looked at it very carefully and then shot back that it couldn't be me, because the person's "praying hands" were too large! That was the only clue that tipped off my own mother. Scary!

Johnny Cash considered *Gospel Road* his "life's proudest work." Nevertheless, he presented "another Jesus." Again, that has to be the case with every attempt to fashion an image of Christ. Dave Hunt wrote his concerns about this in *The Berean Call*:

> The error is even worse when someone dares to portray Christ on the screen. Of himself, Jesus said, "He that hath seen me hath seen the Father" (John 14:9)! What actor playing "Jesus" would dare to say that? Yet they are attempting to portray in their flesh what Paul described as "without controversy, great is the mystery...God was manifest in the flesh..."(1 Timothy 3:16). What audacity! And what of those who watch with approval and are influenced by such portrayals?
>
> After viewing such movies, many sincere people see in their minds the actor who played "Christ" every time they think of Jesus. Does that please our Lord? I will leave that to your conscience.[21]

Our own consciences have been pricked about all of this here at The Berean Call. We've been as guilty as anyone else regarding the use of still "images of Jesus" in our various productions, from our newsletter cover pages to our videos. We've confessed this before the Lord and are in the process of deleting such "production value" visuals from the videos we've produced.

In a previous chapter, the words of Jesus to His disciples were quoted regarding the signs of His second coming. They bear repeating: "And Jesus answered and said unto them, Take heed that no man deceive you. For many shall come in my name, saying I am Christ; and shall deceive many" (Matthew 24:4,5). Might films featuring "Jesus" contribute to that deception? With all the films around that have assorted "Jesuses," won't each one's portrayal contribute to a host of different impressions for the masses? The "Jesus" of the ABC-TV network presentation of *Judas*, for example, confided apologetically to Judas that he "blew it" when he chased the moneychangers from the Temple: "I was trying to make a point. I lost my temper." Later in the movie he turns the money purse over to Judas, admitting, "I'm no good with money. Whatever I have, I tend to lose."

Those character flaws in the One "who knew no sin" (2 Corinthians 5:21) are blasphemous to those who know the Bible. But in these days in which evangelicals are being weaned from the Bible, such discernment may not be that common. Furthermore, what's the difference between an obviously false Christ and a not-so-obviously false Christ? The former may not be as acceptable as the latter—but they will all find an audience. Mel Gibson's and James Caviezel's "Christ" has been enthusiastically promoted by some of the most prominent names in Christendom. "Added touches" by Mel to fill out his personal vision of Jesus were enthusiastically applauded by the shepherds and termed "artistic license." Incredible! The *entire film* is "artistic license." There is not *one* scene in the movie that was not Mel's personal interpretation of the way he sees the scriptural events he selected. He says that time after time in his interviews. That's what movies are: someone's vision adapted to the screen—and, when done well, they have the power to capture hearts and minds.

One email that ended up at my house via the evangelical friend's pipeline (referred to earlier) contained a testimony of a lady who had just seen *The Passion*. She wrote, "That's my Jesus! I came out of the theater last evening, my eyes giving me away, just wanting someone to ask me, so I could answer, 'That's my Jesus! I'm willing to claim him!' Go. Fall in love with Jesus. Adore Him. Worship Him. Don't be afraid to love Him.... Look at Him! Isn't He amazing? Isn't He full of awe?! Come kiss His feet with me as Mary did. Come."[22] Is it James Caviezel she fell in love with, or the true Christ, whom he couldn't portray? The answer is tragically obvious.

Did Mary kiss the feet of Jesus? In the film she did, of course. But that was just another "artistic touch." There were lots and lots of touches involving Mary, which may have been the reason for James Caviezel saying: "This film is something that I believe was made by Mary for Her Son."[23] Does this film, as do the "Church-approved" apparitions of "Mary," promote the "Mother of God" as much or more than they do her Son? Is "Mary" the uncredited "executive producer?" ◀))

MARY, THE EXECUTIVE PRODUCER?

• •

AN "EXECUTIVE PRODUCER" CREDIT on a film is not a title that can be easily defined. Unlike the director, writer, cinematographer, or actor, whose jobs are fairly straightforward and well known, an executive producer's job is often a mystery. Sometimes they are the ones who bring in the money; at other times they gather together the "critical" people. For a movie made entirely on a foreign location, the title may be given to someone who's a native and can cut through the red tape and pull the necessary strings. An executive producer may have a real influence on a film, or, in the case of a well-known producer, "name recognition" may open doors for the project.

So why allude to "Mary" as the executive producer? She seems to fit for two reasons: 1) Mel Gibson's statement to *Christianity Today* editor David Neff that his "film is so Marian" (he "calls Mary co-redemptrix")[24] and, more particularly, 2) James Caviezel's quote that the movie "is something that I believe was made by Mary for Her Son." He prayed the rosary to her continually, beseeching her help. All of that, as well as the inclusion of so many extra-biblical Marian scenes, certainly suggests a superintending influence from Roman Catholicism's Mary. The context of Mel's quote in *CT* had to do with his surprise at the enthusiastic support his "so Marian" film was given by evangelical leaders and pastors: "I've been actually amazed at the way I would say the evangelical audience has—hands down—responded to this film more than any other Christian group."[25] He may be surprised, but I'm shell-shocked, even though I had my suspicions that this was coming.

The appeal of Mary is a growing phenomenon that has spread far beyond the traditional borders of the Catholic and Orthodox Churches. Mary, who has more shrines dedicated to her than any other religious figure (hundreds of times more than her Son!), is rapidly becoming the "queen of ecumenism"— someone whom diverse religions can honor, rally around, and even worship without offending their respective theologies. The *Los Angeles Times* reported that "A growing number of Americans from all Christian denominations are reaching out to the Virgin Mary as a comforting conduit of spirituality and a symbol of peace in troubled times.... It's not just Catholics who are interested in Mary and following the apparitions...."[26]

When an apparition of Mary appears in Islamic countries, multitudes of Muslims turn out to honor her. For example, in the late 1960s, thousands witnessed "a lady composed of light" who was holding a baby as she seemed to hover above the roof of a Coptic Orthodox church on the outskirts of Cairo, Egypt. "Several nights each week, thousands of Moslems (who constituted most of the crowds) fell to their knees on prayer rugs spread wherever space permitted and wept before the 'magnificent, wondrous, glorious form of Our Lady from Heaven'"[27] While such a reaction may seem puzzling to western Christians, there is a substantial basis for it. An entire chapter ("Maryam") in the *Qur'an*, and numerous other verses (more than are contained in the Bible!), as well as hundreds of *hadiths* (books of Islamic sacred tradition) pay homage to Mary, the mother of Jesus.

Islamic scholar Aliah Schleifer writes in her book, *Mary, the Blessed Virgin of Islam,* that Mary is esteemed above the women most revered in the Muslim faith, including Muhammad's wives Khadija and Aisha and his daughter Fatima. Schleifer cites one *hadith* to quote Muhammad saying he would take Mary as one of his wives in heaven: "The Messenger of God said, 'God married me in Paradise to Mary…'."[28] Bishop Fulton J. Sheen, the popular Catholic televangelist of the late '50s and early '60s, predicted that Mary would be the key to reconciling the faiths of Rome and Mecca.

Many of the apparitions of Mary are leading the ecumenical way. "Our Lady of Medjugorje," who, it is claimed, has made numerous appearances in the war-torn area of Bosnia and Herzegovina (where Roman Catholics, Muslims, and Orthodox are still killing one another), allegedly communicated to one of the visionaries, "Tell this priest, tell everyone, that it is you who are divided on earth. The Muslims and the Orthodox, for the same reason as Catholics, are equal before my Son and I [sic]. You are all my children."[29] James Caviezel and his wife are both devoted to Our Lady of Medjugorje. He credits Our Lady for enabling him to play her son: "In preparation, I used all that Medjugorje taught me," as well as a "piece of the true cross" received from one of the visionaries to whom the alleged apparition of Medjugorje appeared.

Mary has played a key role in the conversion of some of the leading Catholic apologists such as Reformed theologian Tim Staples and Scott Hahn (a graduate of the evangelical Gordon-Conwell Seminary and former Presbyterian minister). Staples credits "the Lord and his Mother" for helping him convert to Roman Catholicism. He writes, "I had despised for so long the Catholic belief in Mary's intercession. But...I finally gave in to her loving call, bidding me follow Christ her son wherever he might lead me...."[30] For spiritual assistance in his conversion, Scott Hahn turned to praying the rosary, in which 153 prayers out of 170 are offered to Mary. He writes in his conversion story, "I proceeded to pray [the rosary], and as I prayed I felt more in my heart what I came to know in my mind: I am a child of God. I don't just have God as my Father and Christ as my brother; I have His Mother for my own."[31] Franciscan University, where Hahn is a professor, is a leader in guiding tours to the shrine of "Our Lady of Medjugorje."

More and more Protestants are becoming attracted to Mary. One can find the statue of "Our Lady of Fifth Avenue" displayed prominently at the historic St. Thomas Episcopal Church in New York City. The late John Cardinal O'Connor and Orthodox Archbishop Peter were on hand for its dedication in 1991. Charles Dickson wrote a popular little book in 1996 encouraging a reconsideration of Mary among evangelicals. Titling it *A Protestant Pastor Looks at Mary,* Dickson points out that Luther and Calvin were more agreeable toward Mary than later generations of their followers. He quotes from a letter Luther wrote to the Duke of Saxony: "May the tender Mother of God herself procure for me the spirit of wisdom profitably and thoroughly to expound this song of hers."

The Passion advances Mary, not in an overtly Catholic, Queen-of-Heaven way, but by showing her presence continually in her humanity—as a mother suffering along with her son. Maia Morgenstern told EWTN that she hoped her role as Mary would be a bridge to all religions, simply by revealing Mary as a mother suffering the loss of her child and "in that respect, she speaks for every mother." Mel Gibson concurs: "The way this film displays [Mary] has been kind of an eye-opener for evangelicals who don't usually look at that aspect. [But] they understand the reality of a mother and a son."[32] It will indeed help the cause, but there are still differences to overcome. The Mary of the Orthodox Church was sinless but not conceived immaculately. The Mary of Islam is confused with Miriam, sister of Moses and Aaron, whose father was Amram. She is not the Mother either of God or of the Son of God (because Allah has no son). The Mary of Catholicism was immaculately conceived, is considered to be the Mother of God, remains a perpetual virgin, is revered as a mediatrix between God and man, and is called the "Queen of Heaven." Conservative Catholics such as Gibson and Caviezel also see her as Co-Redemptrix, i.e., she participated in humanity's redemption by vicariously suffering along with her son.

Then there's the Mary of the Bible. The only truth about Mary is found in the Scriptures, presented by those who knew her personally. More importantly, what they had to say was inspired by the Holy Spirit. Fewer than 90 verses address the life of Mary, and in them we find a wonderfully humble servant of the Lord who rejoices in Him as her Savior (Luke 1:47). Obviously, her heart was not "immaculate," nor was she conceived without sin, because her Son—*her Savior*—came not for the righteous but "to seek and to save that which was lost" (Luke 19:10). Mary's ministry was simply giving birth to and nurturing the child Jesus. Once He reached adulthood, she played no part at all in His earthly ministry. It's at the wedding feast of Cana (the beginning of the public ministry of Jesus) where her last words are recorded. Fittingly, she tells the servants, "Whatsoever he saith unto you, do it" (John 2:5). There is no doubt that she is exemplary among biblical saints as a model of obedience and submission to the will of God, especially in the appointment to which she was called. In keeping with the words of John the Baptist, "He must increase, but I must decrease" (John 3:30), Mary faded into the background.

Search the Scriptures as you will and you will find no leadership role for Mary among the Apostles. She taught no doctrine. We never hear of her being sought out for counsel by the Apostles. Other than the gospels, Mary is mentioned only once in the New Testament, and that, the Book of Acts tells us, was in simple participation at a prayer meeting, along with her *sons.* (The teaching that Mary was a perpetual virgin is also contradicted by many other verses—Matthew 12:46; Mark 6:3; John 7:3,5; 1 Corinthians 9:5; Galatians 1:19; Psalm 69:8, et al.).

Remember, nearly all details of the scenes in *The Passion* featuring Mary were provided by three women who were devoted to the Catholic Mary and who received their information through communications with *apparitions*. Mel acknowledges that the Church has not accepted everything written by them. However, taking into consideration only what the Church-approved Marian apparitions say and do, and comparing their statements with the Mary presented in the Scriptures, you get, to borrow a phrase, a Mary "quite contrary." In subtle and sometimes not-so-subtle ways, the apparitions are given to self-aggrandizement and self-promotion—all to the devaluation of Jesus. Consider this communication from "Our Lady of Fatima":

> Say the Rosary every day to obtain peace for the world.... Pray, pray, a great deal, and make sacrifices for sinners, for many souls go to Hell because they have no one to make sacrifices for them.... God wishes to establish in the world the devotion to my immaculate heart. If people do what I tell you, many souls will be saved and there will be peace.[33]

This is not the humble and submissive Mary of the Bible. The rosary invokes prayers to Mary ten to one times more than prayers to the Lord. The Bible tells us that *Jesus* is the Prince of Peace! Only Christ's once-for-all sacrifice saves souls from hell. Neither is Mary's heart immaculate, nor are we to be spiritually devoted to anyone other than our Lord and Savior. Furthermore, the Marian apparitions present a status for Mary that is without precedent and that lacks support in the Scriptures. The Apostle Peter, a contemporary of Mary and regarded by Catholics as the first pope, wrote nothing about her. The Apostle Paul, through the Holy Spirit, gave more specific instruction for living the Christian life than any writer in the Bible, yet made no mention of the alleged importance of devotions or reparations relative to Mary. In contrast to the apparitional Mary, who claims to have been "conceived without sin," Paul called himself "the chief of sinners," yet God made him the most productive figure of the New Testament after Christ. The Apostle John, who wrote the last book of the Bible and was given the care of Mary by Jesus himself, says nothing about venerating her.

The apparitions are clearly *not* of the biblical mother of Jesus, although they make every attempt to be perceived that way. Nearly all show up as a *young* lady bearing an infant, which brings up another crucial question: Who's the child? Jesus was in His early thirties when He ascended into heaven. The obvious implication is that Mary has the *superior* position in the relationship; what small child would not be obedient to his mother? By stark contrast, however, the Bible presents Jesus *not* as a helpless babe, but exalts Him as the King of kings, Lord of lords, Creator of the universe, the glorified Son of God, God manifested in the flesh. In an odd sort of way, Mel paid tribute to the Madonna-and-child apparitions by having *Satan* appear with a miniature, demented creature in "her" arms. He has referred to it as an anti-Madonna, saying that "it's evil distorting good." The problem here is that the Madonna-with-child apparitions, as represented to Catholics down through history in beautiful images, are far more deadly. Yet many evangelicals are blind to that reality. *Christianity Today* notes with approval, "From whatever point in his spirituality Gibson's treatment of Mary is springing, it is touching deeply the maternal impulse of his viewers."[34] Maternal impulse toward *Jesus*? What is *that*?

Unlike the biblical Mary, who faithfully fulfilled her ministry and faded into the background, the Roman Catholic Mary has risen to prominence, drawing millions after herself. *The Passion of the Christ* will whet the appetites of millions more for the Catholic Mary by providing unbiblical "details." Many will turn to the latest apparitions for the "most up-to-date" news about her. Even so, the most serious problem with the movie's extra-biblical scenes featuring Mary is *what they are there for*: to reinforce the Roman Catholic gospel. From scene one, where Mary awakens in great anxiety over the things she knows in her heart will happen that day, to the last scene, where the lifeless body of "Christ" is draped across her own, *The Passion of the Christ* is about the *physical* sufferings of "Jesus" being offered to God for the sins of humanity. Is that what the Bible teaches, or is that "another gospel"? ◀◈

ANOTHER GOSPEL?

• •

SOME CRITICS OF *The Passion of the Christ* dislike it because
of the extreme violence it portrays. A critic from *Newsweek*
called it "the Gospel according to the Marquis de Sade." *The
New Yorker* reported the movie to be "a sickening death trip, a
grimly unilluminating procession of treachery, beatings, blood
and agony." An article in the *Hollywood Reporter* was titled "It's
all about the pain in Gibson's 'Passion.'" He had trouble with
Mel's "focusing narrowly on the 'passion' of Christ—meaning
the suffering and ultimate redemption in the final moments of
Jesus' life." He calls the film a "medieval Passion play with
much better effects. Flesh is flayed in grotesque detail. Body
fluids spurt in exquisite patterns.... [T]he key figure here, Jesus
himself (a game, blood-crusted Jim Caviezel), is such a punch-
ing bag for most of the movie that the filmmakers lose sight of
his message."[35]

Critics are certainly entitled to their opinions, but I don't think the filmmaker lost sight of *his message*.

Nationally known movie reviewer Roger Ebert, who gave *The Passion* his top rating, writes: "The movie is 126 minutes long, and I would guess that at least 100 of those minutes, maybe more, are concerned specifically and graphically with the *details of the torture and death* of Jesus. This is the most violent film I have ever seen" (emphasis added).[36] Ebert said in a final note, "It will probably be the most violent [film] you have ever seen. This is not a criticism but an observation…but [it] works powerfully for those who can endure it."[37]

In what way does the movie "work powerfully"? Movie magic and theology! Mel has ushered the viewer into *his vision* of the sufferings and death of Jesus, which he believes were necessary for a sinful humanity to be reconciled to God. As a gifted filmmaker, he put together everything that he knew to be effective in his medium to best convey (and convince others of) his *theological understanding* of what took place. Yet, sadly, this film misses the punishment for our sins that Christ endured from God and focuses exclusively on the physical sufferings inflicted by men—which could never save, but only condemn us. This tragic misunderstanding is the very heart of the movie and must be corrected by anyone seeking to evangelize those who have been stirred to interest by viewing Gibson's film.

All of this didn't spring from his imagination overnight. He combined his lifetime of experience in Catholicism with his last dozen years of studying the Passion and packaged it in this film. Mel gave some of the background to Ray Arroyo of EWTN:

ARROYO: Talk to me a second about why you decided to restrict yourself to the 12 hours before his death. Why not the ministry? Why not the Resurrection?

GIBSON: Well, for me, that's the most effective part—is the sacrifice—the sacrificial aspect of Christ. And that's where it all comes to a head. [But he misses the true sacrificial aspect!]

ARROYO: And that's what first drew you to the project and wanting to focus on that aspect of Christ's life.

GIBSON: Yes. I'm curious about it, too. I'm like— what is it? I mean, you hear about it. You read about it. It is the central theme of the faith of Christians. I mean, I wanted to find out about it in a complete way—in a full way. And I began to read and investigate about it.

ARROYO: I want to talk for a second about the violence. People have focused on the violence. It is intense. It is graphic at moments. Why did you decide, "I want it to be this brutal?"

GIBSON: I don't think it's as brutal as it really was…. I stopped way short of what I think probably really happened. However, it is brutal. It is graphic. I don't know if anybody under the age of 12 should go and see it. That would be a call that parents would have to make, I think. I don't know—it *should* be shocking.

ARROYO: There is a sense of beauty, though, in the violence, and I don't quite know if that's the right—if I'm expressing that correctly. Do you sense that?

GIBSON: Good! Yes, I do. There's a definite intent to do that—to make it lyrical—to make the violence lyrical, in a way, or to find the beauty in it.

ARROYO: Why was it important for you to depict it in this raw fashion? 'Cause you could have taken a more artistic—you know, a distant glance at this, as we have seen in the past. Why get up-close and personal like this?

GIBSON: Just because it's up-close and personal. I mean, you said it. I want it to be close and personal. And I want the full savagery of it to sort of, like, jump out of the screen at you. And, at the same time—and this is the trick—is to be moved by it, not just repelled by it, but to be moved and drawn in by it—not able to leave. I wanted to do a bunch of things at the same time.

ARROYO: You didn't just throw—slap this together. You spent a lot of time studying flagellations, crucifixions...tell me a little about that study.

GIBSON: Oh, gosh, I mean there's a lot of books you can read on the subject, not the least of which was Anne Emmerich's [*The Dolorous Passion*], in which she talked of these things. It's like, well, vicious. Also, even in more recent times there's medical guides that have sort of gone into it and talked about the physiological aspects of what would happen if someone were tortured and crucified and all this kind of stuff. And there's something called *The Doctor at Calvary* that I read that talked about the asphyxiation and the blood loss and all this—the water from the side—the whole deal, you know? They give it medical terms that doctors can relate to, but that now the layman can read too. It's just very interesting to read all this different material on the matter.

ARROYO: No man could have survived it.

Gibson: No, I don't think so. No, the divine was definitely at work here.[38]

I agree with Mel. The divine was definitely at work—not, however, in the sense in which Mel believes, nor in the focus upon which he has devoted so much of his time, thought, energy, finances, and *faith*. All he sees and attempts to portray is human brutality vented upon Christ, because Catholicism emphasizes *physical* suffering, whether in this life or in purgatory—but the physical cannot pay the penalty for sin.

Let's consider *only* what the Bible says about the matter. Mel says he "believes every word of it," and he notes, regarding visionary Anne Catherine Emmerich's subjective writings, that one doesn't "have to believe any of [them]." So let's let the Bible alone be our guide in this as we go over some basics. The first verse that most Christians commit to memory is John 3: 16: "For God so loved the world, that he gave his only begotten Son, that whosoever believeth in him should not perish, but have everlasting life."

This verse raises some questions that need to be answered: 1) Why does God love us—"the world"? and 2) Why give His Son? The basic answer to number one is: He loves us, not because there's anything lovely in us but because of God's infinite attribute: "God *is* love" (1 John 4:8). Question number two is answered partially within the verse itself. *Believing* in His Son is necessary to avoid perishing (i.e., being separated from God forever) and to gain everlasting life (i.e., being with Him forever).

But that leaves us with some other questions that are critical to a basic understanding of the gospel—the good news of why Jesus came: What's the problem?! What was so serious that God had to send His Son to solve? *Sin.*

The Bible tells us that "*all* have sinned" and "the wages of sin is death" (Romans 3:23; 6:23). Everyone is a sinner; we're all reaping the destruction that sin produces; and, left on our own, every sinner is presently separated from God and will be forever. Mankind has a hopeless problem that he cannot solve. Only God can provide the solution. But why send His Son? Why not just forgive everyone and start fresh? It has to do with God's attributes. One is love, as we've seen, and another is *justice*: God is "a God of truth...*just* and right is he" (Deuteronomy 32:4). God declared to the first man that the penalty for sin is death (Genesis 2:17). The Creator of the universe *set* this penalty, and His perfect justice demands that this penalty—this *infinite* penalty—be paid.

Since every man is a sinner and is therefore under eternal condemnation, there's nothing he can do about the penalty except to pay the eternal consequences. Divine justice must be satisfied. However, God is also love, and in His perfect love He provided the solution for the justly condemned. That's the good news! God became a Man: "And the Word was made flesh, and dwelt among us" (John 1:14); "...the man Christ Jesus" (1 Timothy 2:5) in order to pay the penalty due all humanity. As the Scriptures clearly indicate, Jesus, who is very God and perfect Man, and who will never cease to be God and Man, needed both attributes to be our Savior. He had to become a Man to die physically, and He had to be God in order to pay the infinite penalty that God's perfect justice required.

We can readily understand that Jesus had to die physically, for "without shedding of blood [there] is no remission [of sin]"

(Hebrews 9:22). But since the full punishment includes *spiritual separation* from God forever, our finite minds cannot comprehend how Jesus could pay that penalty on the cross. Yet we know it must be so. Hebrews 2:9 tells us that Christ "by the grace of God should *taste death* for every man." *He became sin for us* (2 Corinthians 5:21), and the wrath of God due every sinner was poured out on Him (John 3:36).

In the three hours on the cross, Christ somehow experienced the punishment due every sinner. Or did he? If He only suffered *physically* and died *physically*, then the "everlasting punishment" due for sin that Jesus spoke about (Matthew 25: 46) wasn't covered. But the words that Jesus exclaimed from the cross tell us that He indeed covered everything: "It is finished!" That term in the Greek, *tetelestai*, was written on bills of sale during the time period of our Lord, and it translates, "Paid in full." Through the full payment by Him, "all that believe are *justified* from *all* things" (Acts 13:39). We were "bought with a price" (1 Corinthians 7:23), and through his *eternal* payment He "obtained *eternal* redemption for us" (Hebrews 9:12). Only an infinite God could pay that price.

The most important "scene" in the Scriptures (as far as revealing the divine penalty that Christ had to suffer) took place in the Garden of Gethsemane. In contrast to the terse and limited accounts (less than ten verses in *all* the gospels directly address His being scourged or crucified) and the scarcity of details regarding His physical sufferings in the gospels, the description of what took place in the Garden is the *only* "up-close-and-personal" revelation of the *suffering* and internal agony of Jesus:

> And he said Abba, Father, all things are possible unto thee; take away this cup from me: nevertheless not what I will, but what thou wilt. (Mark 14:36)
>
> And being in agony he prayed more earnestly: and his sweat was as it were great drops of blood falling down to the ground. (Luke 22:44)

Was Jesus agonizing over the physical suffering that He knew He was about to experience at the hands of men? No. Thousands of men before and after Him suffered scourging and crucifixion—some hanging on their crosses for days in prideful defiance. Were scourging and being nailed to a cross the worst possible tortures men could devise? Not even close. What Christian martyrs experienced during the Inquisition was unspeakably worse. All tortures were designed to cause the most horrific pain and suffering possible while managing to keep the victim alive. Martyrs in Islamic countries have had their bodies roasted and their skin peeled completely off their torsos. Whatever men did to torture Jesus only demonstrated the wickedness of the human heart. It contributed nothing toward satisfying divine justice.

Jesus offered the above prayer three times to "Abba, Father." *Abba* is a very intimate term that is sometimes translated as "Daddy." He knew the price He was about to pay: separation from His Father. Although we can't fathom how great the love that exists between the Father, Son, and Holy Spirit, we get an inkling of it in the reaction of Jesus. His heart agonized so intensely "that his sweat was as it were great drops of blood." But it didn't stop there. He became "sin for us"! It was for us that He suffered the wrath of His Father. It was for our sakes that "it pleased the LORD [Jehovah God] to bruise Him; *he* hath put him to grief" (Isaiah 53:10). Jehovah made "his *soul* an offering for sin" (emphasis added). To comprehend such love is beyond us, but having even a sense of it is enough to fill our hearts with profound gratitude for all eternity.

Between the sixth hour and the ninth hour, darkness descended over all the earth (Luke 23:44), and Jesus cried out (something He never did throughout the physical abuses of scourging and crucifixion!), "My God, my God, why hast thou forsaken me?" (Matthew 27:46). This was when our "ransom" was paid (1 Timothy 2:6). "And when Jesus had cried with a loud voice, he said, Father, into thy hands I commend my spirit: and having said thus, he gave up the ghost" (Luke 23:46). Charles Wesley wrote something wonderful to ponder, but steeped in the mystery of godliness: "Amazing love, how can it be, that thou, my God, shouldst die for me?"

It is clear from the Scriptures that man can have no part in his own redemption. Logic tells us the same. An evangelical friend of mine had a conversation with a nun. She told him they both had much in common, with this one difference: he believed that Jesus paid 100 percent of the penalty for salvation. She believed that Jesus paid 99 percent, and, as a Catholic, she needed to pay the remaining 1 percent. Is that possible? What is one percent of eternal separation from God? She and Mel (as did I, growing up Catholic) focus on a redemption that cannot save them or anyone else. It is a rejection of Christ's unspeakable gift—something that only He could, and did, pay completely. Nevertheless, that's the Gospel of Rome:

> Every man has his own share in the Redemption....
> In bringing about the Redemption through suffering,
> Christ has also raised human suffering to the level of the
> Redemption. Thus each man, in his suffering, can also
> become a sharer in the redemptive suffering of Christ.
>
> —John Paul II, *Salvifici Doloris*, no. 19

In the *Christianity Today* interview with Mel Gibson, the magazine features a quote by Mel giving his misunderstanding of the gospel: "In the Old Covenant, blood was required. In the New Covenant, blood was required. *Jesus could have pricked His finger, but He didn't;* He went all the way"[39] (emphasis added). If Jesus had simply "pricked His finger," we would all still be dead in our trespasses and sins. The full penalty would not have been paid. I can understand Mel not grasping this, but it is reprehensible that a professing evangelical magazine would favorably imply a false gospel.

Is this the sort of teaching that an evangelical would want communicated in his church or Bible study? What about the teachings addressed in the last chapter regarding Mary? What about sending evangelicals to a movie to pick up some of the points? Would that in any way be related to turning the sheep over to a "hireling"? ◀))

SHEEP FED BY
THE HIRELING?

• •

IN NAMING THIS CHAPTER as I did, I thought of the terms in a way that is not totally consistent with the meaning given in John 10:12–14. Therefore, some qualifications are in order. In the parable of the hireling and the good shepherd, Jesus contrasts someone who *owns* the sheep with someone who merely receives wages to watch over them. The point is that there is no real comparison. Although they may share common experiences with the sheep while tending them, the hireling will bolt at the first sign of danger to the sheep, if it adversely affects his own wellbeing. The hireling "careth not for the sheep." The good shepherd, on the other hand, *loves* his sheep, knows them, and even lays down his life for them.

I have only some of the above in mind, as I'll explain. To put it simply, I see Mel Gibson as a hireling to whom the evangelical shepherds have herded their sheep. But that's not really fair to Mel, who wasn't looking for the job of tending the sheep. Of course he wanted them to come see his movie, but no more than he wanted anyone else to come. Yet the sheep showed up in droves that far-and-away outnumbered any other group—thanks to their pastors. Mel was stunned. Remember how he told *Christianity Today* that he was "actually amazed" at the overwhelming support by evangelicals for his "Marian" film? Mel may have taken in a lot of "filthy lucre" from the sheep, but they were not wages; they were more like donations. Nevertheless, without even auditioning for the part, he has *become* a tender/teacher of the evangelical sheep. For example, *Christianity Today* editor David Neff observed: "After both of *The Passion* screenings I attended, the Protestant women talked about identifying with Mary as a mother who was watching her child suffer."[40] Although this is certainly implied in the Scriptures, Mel made the point far more dramatically and with many extra-biblical details thrown in.

Conservative Catholic magazine *Inside the Vatican* acknowledges the valuable ecumenical influence *The Passion* is having:

> For evangelicals, the film has given them a glimpse inside the Catholic soul, even the traditional Catholic soul. Many evangelicals, reflecting on what they saw in the movie, say they are beginning to 'get' the whole Catholic thing: Lent...the ashes on the forehead...no meat on Friday...the sorrowful mysteries...the Stations of the Cross...the emphasis on the Eucharist...the devotion to Mary...the

enormous crucifix hanging above every Catholic
altar. They may not be rushing out to buy rosaries,
necessarily, but some of the things no longer seem so
strange, so alien. (ellipses in original)[41]

On my second viewing of *The Passion*, I tried to identify
the scenes that I thought might have the most dramatic influence
on the hearts and minds of Bible-believing Christians. Though
the movie is one emotionally charged scene after another, when
the screen subtitle presents a verse of Scripture, *the acceptance*
of what is taking place becomes almost irresistible for those
who know and love God's Word. When the *screen Jesus* "says,"
*I am the way, the truth and the life. No man comes to the Father
except through me*, the Word brings instant credibility to the
scene. That seemed to be the effect even in the extra-biblical
scenes. When the screen Jesus fell while carrying his cross and
his mother came to his aid, he reassured her with a verse that the
Bible indicates Christ will not utter until the time of the New
Jerusalem, "Behold, I make all things new" (Revelation 21:5).
Although it's true that God's Word will not return void, it can
also be used as a powerful ploy of seduction just as Satan unsuc-
cessfully attempted to do by quoting Scripture in the temptation
of our Lord (Matthew 4). Every time a Scripture verse appeared
on the screen in *The Passion*, evangelicals around me reacted
enthusiastically. They were believing Mel's vision.

Before we consider Mel's other *teachings* from his movie,
reading quotes from the nationally known shepherds (some of
whom are flirting with being branded "hirelings" themselves)
might be helpful in order to understand why the sheep were so

eager for "showtime." By the way, the quotes I've collected would fill nine pages, so in the interest of the same fairness that I've tried to show Mel, I'll give a few of the quotes without naming the leaders who said them. I don't wish to fill nine pages in this book with all of them, and I don't want to be accused of playing favorites (or unfavorites). Besides, most of the quotes have been used by various promotions for *The Passion of the Christ*, and they can all be found quite easily if anyone is interested. I also took the liberty of printing in **bold type** some things previously discussed, as a reminder.

So let's support [*The Passion*] in every way we can. We should not just wait for it to come out on video, we should see this movie **in droves** at the theater. We should not just go alone, but **in groups** (and especially take unbelievers). We should **not just see it once,** but twice, and we should all buy **the DVD or video**. Let's not just critique culture, **let's actually transform it by being redemptively *involved* in it.**

. . . .

This will do for "Jesus" movies what *Saving Private Ryan* did for war pictures. Every Christian MUST go see this movie and hold Mr. Gibson up in prayer. He's going to take a lot of heat for this project, but if we'll support him, this movie could have a **profound spiritual effect** on millions of people. (caps emphasis in original)

. . . .

Brilliant, **biblical** – a masterpiece.

. . . .

I can't tell you how I admire, respect and applaud you. May God give you the blessing you need, where you need it most. *The Passion* is an awe-inspiring portrayal of the last hours of Jesus' life. It is **an accurate account of Jesus' real sufferings for the sins of the whole world**. This is not a film anyone should miss.

. . . .

The Passion is simply fabulous. It is emotionally wrenching because it is **brutally honest about the violence of Jesus' death**. Never in my life have I seen any movie that comes even close to depicting what Roman crucifixion was really like. Long familiarity and theological explanation have leached out in our minds the awful brutality of Jesus' trial and death. John's simple words, "then Pilate took Jesus and scourged him" **feel vastly different** as you watch two brutal Roman soldiers go on minute after terrible minute bludgeoning Jesus' near-naked body with flesh-gouging whips. Pious talk about Jesus' death for our sins takes on **a whole new meaning**.

. . . .

Every time I preach or speak about the Cross, **the things I saw on the screen** will be on my heart and mind.

. . . .

As President of…I am pleased to voice my strong support for *The Passion*. The [ministry name] sphere of influence includes tens of thousands of staff and volunteers, as well as hundreds of thousands of adults and kids who would be lining up in an instant to see this film. In addition, I think the film will have mass appeal to people of any faith or no particular faith, simply because of the quality of the production and **the historical nature of the content**.

. . . .

Three words summarize for me: Sobering, Stunning, Haunting…. **The details are very accurate—this is the kind of death our Lord died for me.**

. . . .

It has been nearly three weeks since I saw the rough cut of *The Passion*. It is still **impacting my life**. I can't stop thinking about it nor can I stop talking about it. I have never seen a film that has **so affected my life**.

· ·

My hope is that [my young people] will be **captured by the presentation**. I believe they will because it is simply **the telling of God's story**. I am most encouraged by the fact that they will see a **true representation of Jesus**: **fully God** and fully man.

· ·

I am praying that Mel Gibson's movie will have a powerful impact on our culture and that it will appeal to millions of movie lovers who are starving for **a glimmer of honesty** regarding the miraculous and life changing story of the One who died for everyone....

· ·

I was **moved deeply** by the film. In fact, it was **a deep spiritual experience for me**. Without a doubt, it was **the closest experience** I have ever been to actually witnessing the suffering and crucifixion of Jesus Christ.

· ·

The Passion of the Christ is the **most moving** and **memorable portrayal of Jesus Christ** that I have ever witnessed. This **masterpiece**...clearly has been **providentially ordained by God** for such a time as this.

This unbridled enthusiasm from evangelical Christianity for a movie produced by a secular company (or religious organization, for that matter) is unprecedented in history. Moreover, the evangelical shepherds have "put their money where their mouths are"! They've backed up their kudos to Mel by purchasing tickets (some for re-sale) for their sheep in the hundreds of thousands. Theaters were sold out for screenings to church groups for days and weeks. Trailers for the movie were shown at Sunday services. Nationally known pastors were telling their audiences that they had seen the film six and eight times. One told his church members that they needed to keep inviting their neighbors to come with them to see *The Passion* as often as they could. Wow!

Okay, let's take a "30-second time out" away from the din of enthusiasm and consider these questions: Would an evangelical pastor give his pulpit to somebody who just came in off the street? Not if he were a good shepherd. What if the person off the street were someone of worldwide fame? Not if the pastor were a good shepherd. Would this pastor give his pulpit to someone whose religious beliefs were contrary to the beliefs he had taught his sheep? Not if he were a good shepherd. Would an evangelical pastor send his flock across the street to hear a famous actor stand on a soapbox and spout off about his religion? Not if he were a good shepherd. What if, instead of the soapbox on the corner, the "spouting off" was done in Latin and Aramaic at a theater down the street?

It is amazing to me that so many evangelicals seem to be in denial about the Catholic underpinnings of *The Passion of the Christ*. A favorable review in an evangelical apologetics magazine sought to quiet any fears that the movie might have some Catholic influences: "A third concern of some Protestants is the Roman Catholic theology of Mel Gibson, the producer.

On viewing the movie, however, I find that if there is any Roman Catholic influence on the film, it is negligible to the point of irrelevance." *I* left the Catholic Church in protest, so that would make me a "concerned Protestant." On the other hand, it's been hinted to me that *I* just may be reading too much into the film from *my* Catholic background. Maybe I let *my* "negative attitude" color any objectivity *I* may have had. Okay. Since the "underpinnings" that *I* want to review as Mel's foundational "teaching" in the movie is the Catholic devotional of the Stations of the Cross, perhaps I can find some objective confirmation. Roger Ebert should be acceptable. He's a nationally syndicated columnist; he loves *The Passion* (gave it four stars); he understands movies (his business is as a movie critic); and he (as a Catholic) knows Roman Catholicism. He writes,

> Anyone raised as a Catholic will be familiar with the stops along the way; [*The Passion of the Christ*] screenplay is inspired not so much by the Gospels as by the 14 Stations of the Cross. As an altar boy, serving during the Stations on Friday nights in Lent, I was encouraged to meditate on Christ's suffering, and I remember the chants as the priest led the way from one station to another: *At the Cross, her station keeping...Stood the mournful Mother weeping... Close to Jesus to the last.*[42]

I rest my case—momentarily. The Stations, more commonly known as the "Way of the Cross," focus on fourteen key events that Jesus supposedly experienced on the day of His crucifixion while carrying His cross from the Roman Praetorium to Calvary's

SHEEP FED BY THE HIRELING?

hill. Originally, the Catholic faithful journeyed to The Holy Land to follow in the "sorrowful" steps of Jesus, but later they were able to gain the same indulgences (remission of punishments to be paid in purgatory) by kneeling before artistic works of Christ carrying His cross that were erected in their local churches. According to the Catholic Encyclopedia, "there is no devotion more richly endowed with indulgences than the Way of the Cross...."[43] This ritual involves meditating on what took place at each station and praying certain prayers, yet it is not quite as it appears.

There are relatively few devotionals in Catholicism that do not include Mary in some fashion, because she *is* the "Mediatrix of all graces." The Way of the Cross is no different. The song sung at each station is called *Stabat Mater*, meaning "the Mother standing." Each of the twenty stanzas describes *not* what Jesus was going through but the "sorrows" of Mary as *she* "stood and watched." (Read Ebert's quote again.) The song is about Mary. Stanza six asks, *Can the human heart refrain/ From partaking in her pain/ In that Mother's pain untold?* Stanza fifteen pleads, *Virgin of all virgins best /Listen to my fond request/ Let me share thy grief divine*, while stanza nineteen makes this request: *Christ, when Thou shalt call me hence/ Be Thy Mother my defense/ Be Thy cross my victory.* The rest are similar.

Again, this is why Mel Gibson himself calls *The Passion* a "Marian film." Although it focuses on Mel's vision of what Christ endured during those twelve hours of passion, the audience is seeing it *through the eyes of Mary*! Protestant women may be initially drawn to her in empathy, but Catholics know that the sufferings she experienced as she "stood and watched" play a major part in her role as co-redemptrix. Should that worry the evangelical shepherds? Let the shepherd of the Church of Rome calm any such fears:

> Mary's work was to be our co-redemptress, and to mediate for us together with Christ, but of course in subordination to Him. He is the one principle Mediator to whom we owe all. Do not be disturbed by this association of Mary with the redemptive work of Christ. If all Christians are members of Christ, and are called upon, as St. Paul says, to fill up what is wanting to the suffering of Christ, then you can be sure that as Mary, His Mother, was more closely associated with Christ than we are, so *she is more closely associated with His redemptive work*. By a special title, therefore, we call her co-redemptress. We call her "Our life, our sweetness, and our hope." For, in bringing forth Christ she brought forth us to life, she is the model of every virtue, and above all should be the glory of all women; and she is our hope as Eve was our despair. All this tells us what she is for. She is our spiritual Mother in heaven, and she fulfills the duties of a Mother, *winning for us by her intercession that grace of Christ which is life to our souls and which, please God, will mean eternal life in the end.*[44] (emphasis added)

Professor Mark Miravalle of Franciscan University of Steubenville writes, "God willed that the Mother of Jesus participate in this redemptive process like no other creature." He then concludes,

> In *The Passion of the Christ*, Gibson has accomplished a Marian feat no pastor or theologian could achieve in the same way. He has given the world through its most popular medium a portrayal

of a real human mother, whose heart is pierced to its very depths as she spiritually shares in the brutal immolation of her innocent Son. Hers is an immaculate heart, which silently endures and offers this suffering with her Son for the same heavenly purpose: to buy back the human race from sin. Mary Co-redemptrix has been given her first international film debut in a supporting role, and it's a hit.[45]

So, "good shepherds," would you let a "hireling" take your pulpit—one who visually preaches that Mary as Co-Redemptrix is "winning for us by her intercession" the graces that "will mean eternal life in the end," and who offers her suffering "to buy back the human race from sin"?

I hope that evangelicals who are reading this book are beginning to understand that the beliefs and practices of the Roman Catholic Church are at extreme odds with the Word of God, and that the one billion souls who follow their Church's teachings are looking not only to *Mary* to help them win eternal life but to their *good works* as well. The evangelical community has either ignored much of this in the spirit of "tolerance," or has embraced it as the ecumenical thing to do. In both cases, evangelicals have lost their concern for the souls of my kinsmen of the faith of my youth. That didn't seem to be the case more than a quarter-century ago, when evangelicals helped lead me to the Lord. What brought about the change? Well, before the tempest of *The Passion* there was an ill wind called *ECT*.

ECT AT
THE MOVIES?

• •

ABOUT A MONTH PRIOR to seeing *The Passion of the Christ*, I saw another religious theatrical film. The title of the movie was *The Book of Mormon*. Since my later screening of *The Passion* was at the same time of day and played in the very same theater, I thought I'd make some comparisons. First of all, *The Book of Mormon* was a very bad film (though the other six people in the theater—Mormons, I suspect—seemed to enjoy it). Theologically, I found it to be more creative in its use of fiction than *The Passion*. "Artistic license" is not a phrase that would do justice to the content.[46]

However, I wondered why *The Book of Mormon* did not have greater support from the evangelical community. Why didn't the evangelical shepherds send the sheep to feed at that trough? True, it *was* a bad movie. It didn't have Mel Gibson's name attached to it—and it was a *bad movie*. But there had to be something else. Then it dawned on me: it was a *Mormon* film! That would certainly put even the most tolerant of Bible-believing and Bible-teaching shepherds on their guard. But why didn't the same hold true for the *Catholic* movie? For the answer we have to go back to the 1960s.

The Second Vatican Ecumenical Council was opened by Pope John XXIII in 1962 and closed by Pope Paul VI in 1965. It greatly changed the face (but not the dogmatic heart) of Roman Catholicism, especially in the United States. Prior to that council, we Catholics understood that (as the Council of Trent and many of the popes had affirmed) there was *no salvation outside the Church of Rome*. If you were in, you had a good chance of getting to heaven; if you were out, you were bound for hell. As a youth going to Catholic schools, I didn't hang around with hell-bound Baptists, Methodists, Episcopalians, and other Protestants. That changed during my last years of attending public high school. I had them as friends, even though, sadly, I knew they weren't going to make it—not even to purgatory.

For centuries in the U.S., there were fairly rigid barriers between Catholics and Protestants. That's interesting, because the historic approach for spreading Roman Catholicism throughout the world has been to adapt to the spiritual culture of the country. With the exception of the U.S., that approach has been taken for hundreds of years in the rest of the Americas, especially south of our borders throughout Central and South America. For example, Haiti is referred to as "85 percent Catholic and 110 percent Vodoun." The integration of Catholicism with Vodoun is so accepted that Catholic and Vodoun priests co-officiate at some of the public ceremonies in Haiti. "Voodoo" functions begin with Catholic prayers. Catholicism throughout South America is also an amalgam of native religion and Church rituals. The pagan deities that are invoked are given the names of established Catholic saints. So, over the centuries, the effective game plan has been for the Church to simply adjust itself to the religion of the land.

That never happened in the U.S.—no doubt because our religion, or religions, were mostly the offspring of the Reformation, and the Council of Trent cemented that concrete barrier. Four hundred years later, however, when the differences faded and theologians started thinking about them simply as semantic problems, enter Vatican II. In November of 1964, Pope Paul VI proclaimed a decree on ecumenism. Its objective was "the restoration of unity among all Christians." The decree coined a new term for those formerly called "Protestants" by the Church: "separated brethren." The intent was to establish that "all who have been *justified by faith in Baptism* are members of Christ's body, and have a right to be called Christian, and are so correctly accepted as brothers by the children of the Catholic faith"[47] (emphasis added).

The "separated brethren" were ruled acceptable, although they had to have been baptized—preferably as infants. The document proposed that dialogues would be helpful in order to "acquire a more adequate understanding of the respective doctrines of our separated brethren, their history, their spiritual and liturgical life, their religious psychology and general background."[47] The result was "getting to know you" dialogues with various Protestant denominations, from Mennonites to Pentecostals to Baptists. It's interesting to note that, whereas growing numbers of Christians see Catholics simply as other Christians, ecumenical Catholics consider Protestants as lesser *Catholics*. The interfaith discussions gradually progressed from chats to charters. In 1994, an historic document was produced that was the "product of [two years] consultation between Evangelical Protestant and Roman Catholic Christians." Titled "Evangelicals & Catholics Together [ECT]: The Christian Mission in the Third Millennium," its mission goals were Christian unity and co-evangelization. The document declared that "Evangelicals and Catholics are brothers and sisters in Christ" and that as "we enter upon a Third Millennium that could be, in the words of John Paul II, 'a springtime of world missions,'" we must "witness together" to win the world to Christ. In that endeavor, however, ECT cautioned against "sheep stealing," asserting that "it is neither theologically legitimate nor a prudent use of resources for one Christian community to proselytize among active adherents of another Christian community." In other words, it's not right for evangelicals to evangelize Roman Catholics and vice versa.

The participants and endorsers of this and later ECT documents make up a veritable who's-who of the evangelical community: Charles Colson (who originated ECT with Catholic priest Richard John Neuhaus), Bill Bright, J. I. Packer, Pat Robertson, Os Guiness, Richard Mouw, Timothy George, Max Lucado, Richard Land, and others.

A few years ago I attended an ECT conference, "Catholics & Evangelicals in Conversation," held at Wheaton College (regarded as the "Harvard" of evangelical educational institutions). The Cliff Barrow Auditorium in the Billy Graham Center was packed out with an even number of Catholics and Protestants (though only a couple of the latter were there to *protest*). Five Catholic priests (including Cardinal George of Chicago) and two nuns shared the platform with seven evangelicals (including J. I. Packer and Timothy George). All had messages encouraging unity that were enthusiastically received by the crowd.

The Vatican II ecumenical strategy seemed to be making enormous headway. Had Rome changed its gospel or any of its other "infallible" doctrines? No. It cannot. Not without dropping the "infallible" dogma of Papal and Magisterial infallibility. So—we can reasonably conclude which side was changing.

On the last day of the conference, I spent the afternoon roaming the campus and briefly interviewing about 100 evangelical students about their understanding of Catholicism and whether or not they thought Catholics needed to be evangelized. Nearly all said they were familiar with Catholic teachings, yet only *two* students felt that it was necessary to share the gospel with them. "They believe basically the same things we do," was the common refrain. That day was one of my saddest in ministry.

These were friendly, bright, articulate Wheaton students who professed to know the Lord, yet I couldn't fathom what they were telling me. Either these representatives of the "next" evangelical generation did not truly understand Roman Catholicism; or they did, but were apathetic about witnessing to Catholics; or—the most devastating thought—of all: they didn't *understand* the gospel! Not one of them had had any classes at evangelical Wheaton that taught or encouraged them to witness to Catholics. Moreover, nearly all the national evangelical leaders with whom they were familiar seemed to preach "tolerance" of Catholic beliefs and practices, so some students wondered what my problem was.

My problem was, and is, this: I am so thankful that twenty-seven years ago some young evangelicals understood that my Catholicism *couldn't save me*, and they were grieved that I might be separated forever from the One they loved (and who also loved me!). They were faithful to share what they had freely received: "the unspeakable gift" of the Lord Jesus himself.

Although by God's grace I have had opportunities to share what I had freely received, it wasn't until a decade ago that I began in earnest to minister the gospel to the "kinsmen of the faith of my youth." This desire developed out of an attempt to help some small ministries that are dedicated to evangelizing Roman Catholics. Those ministries were taking some heavy hits, thanks to a surge of enthusiasm by ECT, Promise Keepers, Prison Fellowship, Campus Crusade, and a number of other evangelical organizations, to break down the "denominational" barriers between Catholics and Protestants. The "hits" included, for example, cancellations of their speaking dates at churches that had elders who were "into" Promise Keepers,[49] and the loss of donations and other support because of the growing sentiment of "tolerance among Christian brothers and sisters." It was about that time that I helped found Reaching Catholics For Christ (RCFC), a cooperative for ministries (a circle-the-wagons-to-hold-off-the-onslaught sort of endeavor) dedicated to reaching Catholics with the "good news."

ECT at the Movies?

The wagons indeed needed to be "circled," as the ecumenical opposition seemed to be adding more troops and taking more territory:

- Evangelicals and Catholics Together added *Christianity Today* as its herald. Nine *CT* editors, including J. I. Packer and ECT founders Chuck Colson and *Father* Richard John Neuhaus, were signers or endorsers of the ECT documents.

- The Pope visited the Catholic World Youth Rally at St. Louis as evangelical Christian contemporary music groups performed, including Audio Adrenaline, Jennifer Knapp, The Ws, D. C. Talk, and Rebecca St. James.

- Billy Graham Crusades had priests and nuns present as counselors for those who "went forward," redirecting them back to local Catholic parishes.

- Pat Robertson's Regent University had a Catholic bishop celebrate the Mass on campus.

- "The Bible Answer Man," Hank Hanegraaff, declared Roman Catholics to be "foundationally Christian."

- Campus Crusade had practicing Catholics in leadership positions in Ireland.

- James Dobson received an honorary degree from Franciscan University, the leading Catholic school in promoting tours to Medjugorje and Vatican II's version of evangelicalism.

- The Lutheran World Federation signed the *Joint Declaration on the Doctrine of Justification* with the Vatican—with no apologies to Martin Luther, of course.

- Some evangelical leaders went out of their way to excuse the sexual scandal in the Catholic priesthood, a shameful situation that is still having repercussions.

All of these events, and many more, clouded the critical differences between the gospel of Rome and the biblical gospel for the evangelical community.

Evangelicals and Catholics were certainly being blown toward each other. There were gusts here and gusts there. But no one saw the Catholic whirlwind from Hollywood coming. "The Greatest Movie Ever Made!" exclaimed one secular magazine, as it filled its pages from cover to cover with stories on *The Passion.* Catholics came to see *their* film, though not at the insistence of their parish priests, or in numbers comparable to the evangelical community. Nevertheless, it was their movie, and they and the Vatican were quietly thrilled to see evangelicals experience "their Passion." Before *The Passion of the Christ* opened in theaters across the country, a book titled *A Guide to the Passion: 100 Questions About The Passion of the Christ* was doing brisk sales (approaching one million at this writing). One of the writers "sets the record straight":

> As someone involved in the distribution and marketing of the film, I noticed early on the fervor with which many Protestant communities were

> preparing to use the film for evangelistic purposes....
> Yet, for all the sophisticated evangelization
> strategies, the irony is that our Protestant brothers
> and sisters cannot adequately speak to many of the
> issues and questions the film evokes because the film
> is so distinctly Marian, so obviously Eucharistic, so
> quintessentially *Catholic*—as is the New Testament.
> (emphasis in the original)[50]

We've seen that Protestants indeed have gleaned a greater appreciation for the Mary of Roman Catholicism after viewing the film. But how did *The Passion* help evangelicals to better understand the Eucharist, which is an integral part of the sacrifice of the Mass and Catholic salvation? Isn't that a good thing? Isn't this movie the greatest thing that could have happened for the hopes of ECT? Perhaps *The Passion* is the godsend that the "Evangelicals and Catholics Together *mission* of co-evangelism for the third millennium" has been hoping for. But just *who* is evangelizing *whom*, and exactly what sort of salvation are we talking about? ◀))

LIGHTS, CAMERA, SALVATION?

• •

CONSIDERING ALL OF THE MOVIES one has seen, who has not shed tears? Or at least had moist eyes? Or laughed uncontrollably at times? Who hasn't felt outrage? How about fear? Who hasn't jumped out of his seat, or turned away from the screen to avoid the horrible fate one knows is coming? That's all a part of the movie-magic experience.

Sometimes we forget that no matter how realistic a scene in a movie seems, it's not reality. "Seems" is the key word here, because the "reality" is what takes place in one's mind. The filmmaker, along with his creative crew, tries to put the movie elements (scene location, lighting, camera angle, music, special effects, acting, dialogue, and so forth) together in a way that will *convince* the audience that what they are seeing and "experiencing" is real. Everything contributes to the "meaning" the director wants to convey.

Take the selection of the camera angle, for example. One close-up of a nail protruding out of a bloodied hand can be far more effective in communicating *suffering* than a wide-angle of a figure hanging from a cross. An overhead shot says something different about a particular scene than does a low-angle shot. Although visual images are not as objective a means of communication as written words (because words have specific meanings), the choice of camera angles can nevertheless effectively help reveal something important about the scene. Therein lies a significant part of the problem.

In trying to translate what is written in the Bible into a movie scene, *adding to* God's Word cannot be avoided. The Bible does not communicate in terms of the camera angle. That's not a part of the medium of the Word of God. It is, however, essential to telling a film story effectively. When applied to biblical content, the choice of the camera angle is a completely subjective attempt to *convey the meaning* of God-inspired words. Not only are the choices subjective, but the way the resulting shot is interpreted is also subjective. The Bible communicates in words that have definitions common to almost everyone's understanding. Pictures, moving or otherwise, lack that objectivity. A simplified example of this would be a crowd of people standing around in an art gallery gazing at a painting. Everyone's response to the painting is unique, so it generates discussions involving various interpretations. (The saying, "a picture *is worth* a thousand words," would be better stated as "*causes* a thousand words.") But then, in the middle of the lively chats, someone holds up a printed sign for everyone to see. It reads: "FIRE...RUN!!"

No interpretive discussions result. The room clears immediately. The objective message was interpreted objectively.

Besides adding subjective camera angles, the filmmaker *adds* music. The Bible does not use music to communicate its message (though it recommends the use of music for worship). In *The Passion*, however, music is chosen to best convey the mood of each scene, including the heightening of the audience's "theological understanding" of suffering through scourging and crucifixion. Sound effects are *added* to help our senses respond, as we hear weeping off-screen...the flesh-tearing crack of a whip...thunderous crashes as dark clouds roll in. Slow motion makes us feel the anguish of a falling Savior. Our eyes become the passageway to our minds as we are captivated by the image of Satan, personified as a seductive woman, gliding through the crowd. These and many more such film techniques create powerful *emotional* moments for an audience. None of these techniques are incorporated in the Word of God because, as we've seen, the Word is *word* oriented. Jesus said, "Thy word is truth." Movies are make-believe. Sadly, however, the trend is well on its way, as some churches have gone beyond using paraphrases to introducing "Video Bible" into their services. One such program is the *WatchWORD Bible New Testament*. It offers "thousands of scenes, special effects, original music and sound effects," inviting the viewer to "*experience* all 260 chapters, totaling 26 hours on 12 DVDs" (emphasis added).

We noted in an earlier chapter that when we're talking movies, we're talking *drama*—not truth. All filmmakers aspire to orchestrate movie devices in order to *manipulate* the emotions of the filmgoers to their desired end through drama. Although that may have its place in other kinds of films and different forms of storytelling, it's contrary to the communication of the Scriptures. The Word of God is straightforward: it involves inspiration and enlightenment. The Bible was inspired of the Holy Spirit (2 Peter 1:21), and its meaning is understood as the Holy Spirit gives understanding (1 Corinthians 2:10). That's the top and bottom line. Any attempt to work outside of those parameters leads to carnal manipulations that produce fleshly or pseudo-spiritual results. Consider the wide variety of responses to the viewing of *The Passion of the Christ*.

Reports are rampant that life-changing experiences are happening to people who see the movie, both in the theater and afterward. They are supposedly being born again, they are turning their lives around, marriages are being put back together, physical healings are taking place, and foes are being reconciled to one another. The list goes on. If that is truly the case, praise the Lord! But I wonder…are people really being saved by what they saw in the film, or are such testimonies the result of movie-magic-produced catharsis? People sobbed openly at the images of "Jesus" being unmercifully tortured. Powerful stuff—but not the stuff of the Bible. Furthermore, Mel Gibson got most of it from *The Dolorous Passion of Our Lord Jesus Christ*, and the author of that book got it from a spirit entity. But couldn't viewing this movie bring strong conviction to the hearts of the millions of viewers who became emotionally sympathetic as they identified with "Jesus" and his sufferings for mankind's sake? If they truly believed what they saw, couldn't they have a born-again experience?

Let's give that some thought. Is what they saw the truth? Or is it what Mel Gibson orchestrated for them to see? Does the Holy Spirit work through the manipulation of emotions, or is it *the truth* that sets one free? When someone truly believes the gospel, emotions may (or may not) be involved, but never as a conditioning device to "ripen" someone to accept Christ. That would be deception and is therefore directly at odds with the Spirit of Truth. Again, nothing on the screen is the work of the Holy Spirit; it is *the craftsmanship of Mel Gibson* and his creative associates. As artistic as the movie may be, it is still *false* in its witting or unwitting pretense to portray Christ and what took place during the hours before His death and resurrection. Therefore, if anyone gets saved due to viewing *The Passion*, it is simply because God has been gracious in His mercies—not because the film provided the biblical gospel of salvation. In fact, it does not!

What *The Passion* does provide is the gospel according to *Rome*. As we've seen, the film demonstrates that it was through "Christ's" physical sufferings, along with Mary's suffering vicariously with him (as "Co-Redemptress"), that the eternal payment for mankind's sins was "accomplished" (the term used in the film's subtitles). This opened the way to heaven for all who would enter in through the Sacrament of Baptism, which isn't included in the film, unless, of course, the "good thief" is credited with what Rome recognizes as the waterless "baptism of desire." As "Jesus" hangs upon the cross, Mel introduces the most significant scenes related to the process of salvation in Roman Catholicism. He uses the visual technique of "flashbacks"

—cutting from a scene in present screen time to a scene of an earlier event—to establish the connection between the Eucharistic Last Supper and "Christ" dying on the cross.

The Roman Catholic Church teaches that Christ instituted the Eucharist (the "Sacrament of Sacraments") at the Last Supper as He changed the bread into His body and the wine into His blood. It also teaches that Jesus ordained His disciples as priests to do the same. Here is what supposedly took place then and continues to the present: "In the most blessed sacrament of the Eucharist 'the body and blood, together with the soul and divinity, of our Lord Jesus Christ and, therefore, *the whole Christ is truly, really, and substantially* contained'" (emphasis in the original).[51] The Eucharist is "a sacrifice because it *re-presents* (makes present) the sacrifice of the cross."[52] This is the most important Sacrament in the *process* of salvation, because it is the way Catholics can obtain sanctifying grace and further justification: "Communion with the flesh of the risen Christ, a flesh 'given life and giving life through the Holy Spirit,' preserves, increases, and renews the life of grace received at Baptism."[53]

When Jim Caviezel reported that he couldn't play Christ without having Christ in him, he believed that he accomplished this by ingesting "Christ" daily into his stomach through the Eucharist. His Church teaches that "partaking of the Body and Blood of Christ has no less an effect than to change us into what we have received."[54] So, did this mode of salvation really make it to the screen? Let's take Mel Gibson's word for it as he comments on the flashback to the Last Supper:

> I think to interrupt the crucifixion with the Last
> Supper is, to me, the most natural thing in the
> world—to go from the offering of the bread and
> the wine, and the body and the blood, to the literal
> bloody sacrifice of the cross—to go to the *unbloody*
> *sacrifice* in the Last Supper is symbolic—it's ritual—
> it's at the heart of Catholicism.[55] (emphasis added)

Rome teaches that at the Mass a sacrificial "re-presenta-tion" of what took place at Calvary occurs: "For in the sacrifice of the mass our Lord is immolated [killed as in a sacrifice] when 'he begins to be present sacramentally as the spiritual food of the faithful under the appearances of bread and wine.'"[55] What's wrong with this? Briefly, the Eucharist is *unbiblical, irrational, and immoral*. The Bible teaches that celebrating "the Lord's supper" is a *memorial service* of thankfulness for the salvation He provided through His death, burial, and resurrection. The Eucharist is *irrational*, because the Roman Catholic Church teaches that Jesus instituted it Himself at the Last Supper, and therefore He must have changed the bread into *His own* body and then "immolated" Himself in a "sacrificial *re-presentation*" even *before* He went to the cross. Is this, then, a *pre-presentation* of a *re-presentation*? And finally, on a *moral* note on Mel's part, the flashback scene of the Last Supper shows "Jesus" drinking his own "blood" on screen. This the Scriptures condemn.

One promotional endorsement for the film was a shocker beyond the rest of the already-shocking list, because it indicated a commitment on the part of the shepherds to the medium of film without regard to the sensitivities of the sheep. This popular author/pastor (among many pastors who showed the trailer in their churches) sent this to Mel Gibson's production company, which is aptly named "Icon":

> Thank you for allowing our congregation to preview the movie trailer of *The Passion*. In just four short minutes, the *image* and the *authenticity* left our members *"spellbound." Something went right to the heart* of those who watched the trailer. (emphasis added)

It is now a fact of life that Mel Gibson's movie is in the church, and the church is into Mel Gibson's movie. That's not to say that every evangelical is "into" it or that there aren't churches that decided against purchasing blocks of tickets or promoting it, though they are a small percentage. We at The Berean Call have heard from thousands with diverse opinions about the film through a questionnaire on our website. I and others on the TBC staff have had conversations with hundreds since screenings of *The Passion*, and we have found that, no matter what disturbing (or worse) information is presented about the movie, the seemingly programmed response is:

"Yes, but…the Lord can still use it."

Let's think seriously about that one. ◀》

YES, BUT...
AND BEYOND

• •

I'VE BEEN TOLD THAT *The Passion of the Christ* is here to stay, so I'd better get used to it—or, better yet, quit nitpicking and use it to win souls for Christ. Good friends who love the film (and they still love me and I still love them, by the way) tell me that thousands of the hundreds of thousands of evangelicals who have seen it (and many who haven't!) are doing their utmost to take advantage of the possibilities it may provide to witness to friends, neighbors, and acquaintances who have seen it, or who have an interest in seeing it.

One enthusiastic pastor from my "grab bag of evangelical-promoters' quotes" remarked, "I have no doubt that the movie will be one of the greatest evangelistic tools in modern day history. I think people will go to it and then flood into the churches seeking to know the deeper implications of this movie." A well-known, very evangelization-oriented parachurch organization agreed: "*The Passion of the Christ* represents an evangelistic opportunity that is unlikely to be repeated in our lifetime."

That's heavy stuff. I'm an evangelical. In all honesty before the Lord, the last thing I would ever want would be to stand in the way (intentionally or unintentionally) of something He's doing. Not that I haven't personally missed the mark on occasion. But in the face of "On this one, Tom, you've missed the mark, the barn, and the county," I need to borrow the phrase that's been quoted to me continuously: "Yes, but...."

Yes, but... what about all the information, reasons, arguments, and concerns I put forth? "I know, but...beside all that...the Lord is using the film in a mighty way. I can't believe you can't see the work of the Holy Spirit in it!"

Stories abound about the Holy Spirit at work on *The Passion* project. Healings were claimed on the set, conversions and turned-around-lives took place, Caviezel's life was spared after being hit by lightning, spiritual battles were won, Mel was "guided" to rich resource materials from nuns claiming mystical visions, he "was moved by the Holy Spirit" while directing, and the evangelical church showed up *en masse* to buy tickets. It's hard to argue with some of that testimonial "proof." But let me see if I can add more meat to their "God had to be involved" premise here. This is an honest, no-kidding attempt to *imagine* a best-case scenario that might indicate that the hand of God is in this.

Let's say that I wanted to communicate the gospel to everyone in the world. What would be the best medium for that?

Movies. Nearly everyone the world over will watch a movie. But there are already a number of movies with gospel content around. What if I could get one of the top box-office stars in Hollywood involved? That would help. And what if he were an Academy Award-winning director as well? Fantastic, but how many of those are there? Now here's an item: What if he had a *passion for Jesus*? Too much! But...a really spectacular film would cost a large chunk of money, and I just don't see the major studios going for it. What if this world-renowned superstar and award-winning director who says he loves Jesus were to put up $30 million of his own money? Now we're talking *miraculous*!

It does seem impressive. But according to whose economy? That sounds like the best laid plans of men and moviemakers. Is it the way God works? Where in the Scriptures do we find an example of God using the "best possible worldly scenario" to further His kingdom or spread His gospel? Doesn't He use the foolish and weak things of the world to confound the wise? And why is that? So that "no flesh should glory in His presence" (1 Corinthians 1:27-29). Gideon's troops were reduced from an overwhelming 32,000 to a "hopeless" 300, so that the glory in the coming victory would belong to God alone (Judges 7). Paul writes that he avoided man's wisdom that the power of God might be manifest (1 Corinthians 2:4,5).

We've reviewed the problems with "the best possible medium to reach the most people" and found it wanting regarding *communicating* the Scriptures. God's Word itself says, "Hath not God made foolish the wisdom of the world? For after that in the wisdom of God the world by wisdom knew not God, it pleased God by the foolishness of *preaching* to save them that believe" (1 Corinthians 1:20,21).

Yes, but....

The wisdom of the world is seen to be all the more foolish when "supplementing" Scripture: the ludicrous scene in the movie in which a Catholic Saint (Veronica) blots the bloodied face of "Jesus," thereby capturing for posterity the image of Jesus on her veil (which served as the model for future images of "Jesus." Mel, incidentally, used the Shroud of Turin for his one-eyed "Jesus" inspiration); or perhaps the raven pecking out the eye of the crucified thief as punishment for his rejecting "Jesus"; and then there's "Jesus," the carpenter, building a state-of-the-art (for the time) table. All of this is man's "wisdom" at work, which is worldly foolishness at best.

Yes, but....

On October 16, 1555, Nicholas Ridley and Hugh Latimer were burned at the stake. Their crime: They told a commission formed by Mary, Queen of England, who was trying to bring England back under the Church of Rome, that they could not accept the abomination of the Mass as a sacrifice of Christ. Latimer explained to his judge/executioners, "Christ made one oblation and sacrifice for the sins of the whole world, and that a perfect sacrifice; neither needeth there to be, nor can there be, any other propitiatory sacrifice." We might well remember Latimer's last words to Ridley: "Be of good comfort, Master Ridley, and play the man. We shall this day, by God's grace, light such a candle in England as I pray shall never be put out." Has that candle almost gone out?

Ridley and Latimer were just two among *tens of thousands* who died horrendous deaths for rejecting what *The Passion* glorifies on the screen, and for what millions of evangelicals are paying to see. Is this the sort of thing that God overlooks as He "uses the movie" to bring in the lost sheep? Or is it His sheep that are being fleeced here?

One final "Yes, but..." consideration: Who says that thousands are being won to Christ due to the witnessing activity surrounding *The Passion of the Christ* or from the power of seeing the film itself? Certainly, there was a great deal of excitement in anticipation of soul winning generated by evangelical Christian leaders who attended pre-release screenings. Honestly, months prior to the movie's release, the great anticipation regarding how the Lord would use *The Passion* reminded me of similar talk during the year prior to the turn of the millennium regarding the expectations about Y2K. The church would rise to the potential crisis and use it to God's glory! The Y2K catastrophe never materialized, obviously, and many Christians were devastated financially and spiritually because of the "how we're gonna use this" hype and a lack of discernment on their part. We're still waiting to see "how the Lord will use" Mel Gibson's movie.

For all of my critical concerns, I take a back seat to no one when it comes to being thankful for every soul that, by God's mercy and grace, receives the gift of eternal life through having been influenced by anything even remotely connected with *The Passion of the Christ*. At the same time, my heart grieves over the far-reaching problems that will result because of this film, much of which I alluded to in this book. You see, beyond the conversion possibilities hoped for by "Yes, but…," there is the more extensive reality of false teachings and shipwrecked faith. In other words, who is going to "fix" the spiritual damage generated by Mel Gibson's visionary movie?

Let's do a brief review, combined with some added thoughts in the light of "spiritual damage control." Roman Catholic apologists understand that *The Passion* is their movie and they expect it to usher in a tremendous renewal for their scandal-ridden Church. They foresee a great increase in former Catholics returning to the flock from evangelical pastures. Also, *The Passion* shifts Catholic efforts toward evangelization into the highest gear perhaps in the history of the Church. Likewise, thanks to the film, Evangelicals and Catholics Together cooperative efforts will gain heretofore unheard of successes.

Reaching Catholics with the biblical gospel, which is normally fraught with difficulties, is now faced with even more intensive oppositions from both ecumenically minded evangelicals and Roman Catholics. Even those evangelical pastors who *know* the problems with Catholicism are fading under the pressure. For example, one of the few pastors I read about who expressed a couple of reservations about *The Passion* to his congregation hinted at one concern: "the accents of Mel Gibson's *denomination*." He didn't say what that denomination was. Why not? There has been a reluctance to mention "Roman Catholicism" from evangelical pulpits throughout Christendom for fear of "offending," and that will certainly increase.

The movement toward the subjective and away from the objective Word of God is rampant in Christendom. We have seen the trend in Bible "translations" move away from the literal versions to the subjective paraphrases (Eugene Peterson's *The Message*, Kenneth Taylor's *The Living Bible*, etc.), and then to the even more *feelings-oriented* medium of film as a means of presenting the Bible visually. One well-known Evangelical author, who has been stumping for *The Passion* in documentaries and on Christian college campuses, declared that the written Word of God was no longer effective for this generation. He said that his children were into visuals and that was the best way to reach them and their friends.

Mel Gibson's contribution in all of this is to portray on the screen his personal meditation: "I think of [*The Passion of the Christ*] as *contemplative* in the sense that one is to remember (unforget) in a spiritual way which cannot be articulated, only *experienced*" (emphasis added).[57] In his EWTN interview, notice how he explains his purpose:

> GIBSON: And I didn't want to have to depend on the spoken work—it's a *visual art* film, and I wanted to take the verb away from it a little bit. Have it there, yeah, but to restrict the spoken word.
>
> ARROYO: You were more interested in, it seems to me, a visceral—you wanted a visceral reaction [characterized or proceeding from instinct rather than intellect] from the audience, and you didn't want the words getting in the way.
>
> GIBSON: That's right. Yeah....

Gibson's screen imagery attempts to introduce content into the minds of the audience, upon which they can meditate, just as do the images in the Stations of the Cross during the ritualistic Catholic devotional. *Christianity Today* seemingly endorses this, noting that the "Christian" roots of this technique stem from a form of "Cross-centered prayer" practiced by mystics in the Middle Ages: "Long before evangelicals like Richard Foster [a *CT* editor and author of *Celebration of Discipline*] began to experiment with *guided imagery* in prayer, those devotional practices also invited believers to place themselves *in their imaginations* into biblical stories"[58] (emphasis added). The magazine adds, "Ignatius [Loyola, founder of the Jesuits] wrote in his widely used *Spiritual Exercises* a set of directions on how to place oneself *imaginatively* [through guided visualization] in the scene of Christ's crucifixion"[59] (emphasis added).

This is all part of a renewal of Catholic mysticism that is making great inroads into evangelical Christianity. A leader in this movement is Richard Foster's organization, *Renovaré*, which will release the *Spiritual Formation Study Bible* (New Testament, edited by Eugene Peterson—a speaker at *Renovaré* conferences), early in 2005. This "contemplative" approach is also impacting young Christians through the efforts of Catholic mystic and former priest Brennan Manning (*The Ragamuffin Gospel*), and *Group Magazine's* Mark Yaconelli, who wrote an article subtitled "How Spiritual Exercises Can Change Your Kids" (see *TBC*'s "Please Contemplate *This*" at www.thebereancall.org for further explanation and documentation). Evangelical *Youth Specialties* seems to be putting it all together for our kids:

Meditating on the events of Jesus' final days and his resurrection can be profound. The challenge for most of us is shutting out the noise and distractions of everyday life long enough to quiet our souls and listen to the Spirit of God.

Here's how you can set up an inspiring means to interactively meditate on Jesus Journey to the Cross: create stations for contemplation around your facility. It's perfect if you have side rooms, stairs, pews, choir loft, and a balcony, but you can be creative and adapt to any situation.

You can offer Journey to the Cross any time of the year. Holy Week can be especially effective. Use it during camp, a lock-in, or a midweek gathering. This design has 13 stations, most of which can accommodate approximately three people at a time.[60]

The popularity of *The Passion* has caused the TV networks to resurrect and air every "religious" film they can dredge up. This means that—from the epics of the 1950s and '60s to the *Jesus Christ, Superstar* musical of the '70s, to the psycho-bio-blasphemous *The Last Temptation of Christ* of the '80s, to the *Judas* and *Jesus* TV releases of this millennium—many "Christs" abound for the choosing. In the "sanctified" name of *artistic license*, filmmakers have turned the biblical Christ into whatever their imaginations conjure up.

Who can honestly say that Mel Gibson's extra-biblical "insights" into Christ are any more valid than Martin Scorsese's in *The Last Temptation of Christ*, other than the fact that the latter's insights were thoroughly repugnant. The damage control issue, however, is figuring out how to help the biblically illiterate to sort out the hosts of false Christs, with whom they are now being—and will be—bombarded.

The problems *beyond* "yes, but…" should not be lost on those who want to win souls to Christ. The Jesus of *any* movie presents a Jesus who is not the Jesus of the Bible. The screen Jesus is a creation of man—not the revelation of the Holy Spirit. As a creation of man, the screen Jesus will teach many false things about the biblical Jesus. The screen Jesus becomes one of the many false Christs who the biblical Jesus said would deceive many. The screen Jesus is a false image that people will carry in their minds. The screen Jesus is an image that manipulates people through their emotions. And the screen Jesus is an image that a jealous God will not tolerate.

What about the screen Jesus for evangelicals who are *somewhat* biblically knowledgeable? One would think that it would be less of a problem for them because they have more content upon which to base their discernment. Yet the screen Jesus seems to be winning, in many cases. The trend toward visually interpreting the Scriptures (which necessitates adding the subjective elements discussed earlier) is a process of weaning viewers from the Word of God as the Holy Spirit inspired it. Personal surveys among those who said they had a fairly good knowledge of the Bible demonstrated that many scenes presented in *The Passion* were believed to be biblical, when they were, in fact, the product of Mel's imagination and the at-best questionable visions of his mystical nuns! Biblical confusion at the very least is on the rise for this *visually fed* evangelical generation.

Even if a best-case "Yes, but..." scenario of conversions results, the church will still be left with spiritual damage control. Among the hopes and prayers that accompany the writing of this book is that the church will take seriously the concerns I've tried to communicate and will *preach and teach* God's Word, God's way.

My voice in this is simply one of many crying in the wilderness. Of the many others, there is one who spoke to these very issues a half-century or so ago, and I believe he did so with insights from the heart of God. Therefore, I'd like to glean some gems from his godly wisdom and present them in the final pages. His name was A. W. Tozer. ◀))

MAN'S WAY OR
GOD'S WAY?

• •

YOU MAY NOT AGREE with most of the concerns I've presented here, but since you've gotten this far, I hope we can come to one point of complete agreement: *we want only what God wants*. We want to do things *His way*, not the way *we think* might further His kingdom. I believe we desire to take heed to the verses (repeated twice, no doubt for emphasis) in the Book of Proverbs: "There is a way which seemeth right unto a man, but the end thereof are the ways of death" (14:12; 16:25). If we are on that same page, then it also may be that we have the same love for the Word of God and therefore have a firm basis for knowing God's way. The Word is the only objective resource we can have to help us figure out what His Way is. If we turn to anything else, we are saying that the Scriptures are insufficient. Yet Peter tells us that in His Word God has "given unto us *all things* that pertain unto life and godliness, through the knowledge of Him…" (2 Peter 1:3). The Apostle Paul writes an exhortation of the same truth to young pastor Timothy: "All scripture is given by inspiration of God, and is profitable for doctrine, for reproof, for correction, for instruction in righteousness: That the man of God may be perfect [mature in the faith], throughly furnished [equipped] unto all good works" (2 Timothy 3:16,17).

God's Word is *sufficient*! It says so. My greatest fear, then, is that the Body of Christ will lose sight of that critical truth. To the degree that we are blinded to that, we have drifted from God's course. Or it may be that we've drifted into an ungodly current that will swell into a torrent, taking many past the "point of no return."

A.W. Tozer has been called a "prophet of the 20th century." I rather doubt that he would personally appreciate that posthumous accolade. His godly humility would forbid it. Nevertheless, the following quotes bespeak a prophet in their spiritual insight and stunning foresight. I remember reading somewhere that he said that he had preached his way out of most of the pulpits in this country. (In other words, he preached the message God put on his heart, and he was not invited back.) Tozer's assessment certainly has a prophet's ring to it! Here are some issues that deeply troubled his soul regarding the intrusion of religious movies into the church in the mid 1950s.

On the necessity of following God's Word exactly, with no additions:

When God gave to Moses the blueprint of the Tabernacle He was careful to include every detail; then, lest Moses should get the notion that he could improve on the original plan, God warned him solemnly, "And look that thou make them after their pattern which was shewed thee in the mount" (Exodus 25:40). God, not Moses, was the architect. To decide the plan was the prerogative of the Deity. No one dare alter it so much as a hairbreath.

The New Testament Church also is built after a pattern. Not the doctrines only, but the methods are divinely given.... [W]hen the New Testament canon was closed, the blueprint for the age was complete. God has added nothing since that time.[61]

On the medium God chose to communicate to us:

It is significant that when God gave to mankind His great redemptive revelation He couched it in words. "And God spake all these words" very well sums up the Bible's own account of how it got here. "Thus saith the Lord" is the constant refrain of the prophets. "The words that I speak unto you, they are spirit and they are life," said our Lord to His hearers (John 6:63). Again He said, "He that heareth my word, and believeth on him that sent me, hath ever lasting life" (John 5:24). Paul made *words* and *faith* to be inseparable: "Faith cometh by hearing, and hearing by the word of God" (Romans 10:17).

Surely it requires no genius to see that the Bible rules out pictures and dramatics as a media for bringing *faith* and *life* to the human soul. The plain fact is that no vital spiritual truth can be expressed by a picture.... Words can say all that God intends them to say, and this they can do without the aid of pictures.[62]

On the use of entertainment to teach spiritual truth:

I believe that most responsible religious teachers will agree that any effort to teach spiritual truth through entertainment is at best futile and at worst positively injurious to the soul....

Religious movies, by appealing directly to the shallowest stratum of our minds, cannot but create bad mental habits which unfit the soul for the reception of genuine spiritual impressions.[63]

On emotional experiences in religious movies:

Religious movies are mistakenly thought by some people to be blessed of the Lord because many come away from them with moist eyes. If this is proof of God's blessing, then we might as well go the whole way and assert that every show that brings tears is of God....

The religious movie is sure to draw together a goodly number of persons who cannot distinguish the twinges of vicarious sympathy from the true operations of the Holy Ghost.[64]

On the "Yes, but...God is using it to His glory" response:

The plea that all this must be good because it is done for the glory of God is a gossamer-thin bit of rationalizing which should not fool anyone above the mental age of six. Such an argument parallels the evil rule of expediency which holds that the *end is everything* and sanctifies the means, however evil, if only the end will be commendable.[65]

On the appeal to the historic use of Miracle, or Passion, Plays in the Church:

Those who would appeal for precedent to the Miracle [Passion] Plays have certainly overlooked some important facts. For instance, *the vogue of the [play] coincided exactly with the most dismally corrupt period the Church has ever known*. When the Church emerged at last from its long moral night these plays lost popularity and finally passed away. And be it remembered, *the instrument God used to bring the Church out of the darkness was not drama; it was the biblical one of Spirit-baptized preaching*. Serious-minded men thundered the truth and the people turned to God.[66]

On the spread of religious drama to evangelical churches:

Can it be.... [t]hat the appearance of the religious movie is symptomatic of the low state of spiritual health we are in today? I fear so. Only the absence of the Holy Spirit from the pulpit and lack of true discernment on the part of professing Christians can account for the spread of religious drama [throughout] so-called evangelical churches. A Spirit-filled church could not tolerate it.[67]

On the necessity of demonstrating scriptural support for biblical movies:

Every sincere Christian must find scriptural authority for the religious movie or reject it, and every producer of such movies, if he would square himself before the faces of honest and reverent men, must either show scriptural credentials or go out of business....

The movie is not the modernization or improvement of any scriptural method; rather it is a medium in itself wholly foreign to the Bible and altogether unauthorized therein.[68]

More words on the sufficiency of the Scriptures:

The whole preach-the-gospel-with-movies idea is founded upon the same basic assumptions as modernism—namely, the Word of God is not final, and that we of this day have a perfect right to add to it or alter it whenever we think we can improve it....[69]

To harmonize the spirit of the religious movie with the spirit of the sacred Scriptures is impossible.... Let a man dare to compare his religious movie show with the spirit of the book of Acts. Let him try to find a place for it in the twelfth chapter of the First Corinthians.... If he cannot see the difference *in kind*, then he is too blind to be trusted in leadership in the church of the Living God....

But some say, "We do not propose to displace the regular method of preaching the gospel. We only want to supplement it." To this I answer: If the movie is needed to supplement anointed preaching it can only be because God's appointed method is inadequate and the movie can do something which God's appointed method cannot do.[70]

On the overwhelming approval of the religious movie:

One thing may bother some earnest souls: why so many good people approve the religious movie. The list of those who are enthusiastic about it includes many who cannot be written off as borderline Christians. If it is an evil, why have these not denounced it?

The answer is, *lack of spiritual discernment....* Now we are paying the price of our folly. The light has gone out and good men are forced to stumble around in the darkness of the human intellects.[71]

On what we should do about being invaded by the spirit of Hollywood:

Let us not for the sake of peace keep still while men without spiritual insight dictate the diet upon which God's children shall feed.... Unity among professing Christians is to be desired, but not at the expense of righteousness. It is good to go with the flock, but I for one refuse mutely to follow a misled flock over a precipice....

If God has given wisdom to see the error of religious shows we owe it to the Church to oppose them openly. We dare not take refuge in "guilty silence." Error is not silent; it is highly vocal and amazingly aggressive. We dare not be less so. But let us take heart: there are still many thousands of Christian people who grieve to see the world take over. If we draw the line and call attention to it we may be surprised how many people will come over to our side and help us drive from the church this latest invader, the spirit of Hollywood.[72]

Thus spoke A.W. Tozer fifty years ago, and although some indeed took to heart his concerns back then, his prophetic message to the church was gradually washed aside in the wake of enthusiasm for the world's ways. I mentioned earlier that Tozer would have objected to being labeled a prophet, even though he knew the future outcome of what was taking place in his day. His objection likely would have been that some might conclude that his words were specific revelations from God rather than a matter of basic biblical math. He simply added up those things contrary to God's Word that were taking place in the church of a half-century ago and accurately projected the results. His conclusions were doubtless influenced also by the way the Bible characterizes the last days of the church preceding the Coming of the Lord Jesus Christ—days in which the numbers of those *falling away from the faith* would proliferate.

Jesus said, "[W]hen the Son of man cometh, shall he find faith on the earth?" (Luke 18:8). Revelation 13 indicates a one-world religion will arise that will feature the worship of the Antichrist. The astounding development of ecumenism throughout Christendom is making this a reality within the church today.

Dave Hunt, in his book *A Woman Rides the Beast* tells us how this is happening:

> The prefix "anti" comes from the Greek language and has two meanings: 1) opposed to, and 2) in the place of or a substitute for. Antichrist will embody both of these meanings. He will indeed oppose Christ, but in the *most diabolically clever way* it could be done: by pretending to be Christ and thus perverting "Christianity" from within. Indeed, Antichrist will "sit in the temple of God showing himself that he is God". (2 Thessalonians 2:4)
>
> If Antichrist pretends to be Christ and is worshiped by the world (Revelation 13:8), then his followers are of course "Christians." [It follows, then, that] Christianity will take over the world, and not real Christianity but an Antichrist counterfeit thereof. Thus, the Great Apostasy precedes the revelation of Antichrist (2 Thessalonians 2:3). Part of the apostasy is the ecumenical movement, which is literally setting the stage for a union between all religions and even influences evangelicals as well. An Antichrist "Christianity" must be created which embraces all religions and which all religions will embrace—precisely what is occurring today with astonishing speed.[73]

How powerful will the deception be? The Gospel of Matthew characterizes it this way: "For there shall arise false Christs, and false prophets, and shall shew great signs and wonders; insomuch that, if it were possible, they shall deceive the very elect" (Matthew 24:24). Paul writes in his second letter to the Thessalonians concerning the Antichrist and those deceived by him, "…whose coming is after the working of Satan [who transforms himself into an "angel of light"–2 Corinthians 11:14] with all power and signs and lying wonders, and with all deceivable-ness of unrighteousness in them that perish; because they received not the love of the truth, that they might be saved. And for this cause God shall send them strong delusion, that they shall believe a lie" (2 Thessalonians 2: 9-11).

How, then, can any believer remain steadfast in the faith and avoid the bondage that such deception will produce? Jesus tells us how, in John 8:31,32: "If you continue in my word, then ye are my disciples indeed; And ye shall know the truth, and the truth shall make you free." Having a love for the truth (He is the Truth—John 14:6), and abiding in His Word (His Word is truth—John 17:17) is God's only way for us to keep ourselves from the "strong delusion" of man's way in these last days.

My prayer is that we who truly love the Lord and His church will do our utmost to heed the Apostle Paul's grieving exhortation to his beloved brothers, the leadership in the Ephesian fellow-ship: "For I have not shunned to declare unto you all the counsel of God. Take heed therefore unto yourselves, and to all the flock, over which the Holy Ghost hath made you overseers, to feed the church of God, which he hath purchased with his own blood. For I know this, that after my departing shall grievous wolves enter in among you, not sparing the flock. Also of your own selves shall men arise speaking perverse things, to draw away disciples after them. Therefore watch, and remember, that by the space of three years I ceased not to warn every one night and day with tears" (Acts 20:27-31). ◁))

EPILOGUE

* *

*For I have not shunned to declare unto you
all the counsel of God.*

*Take heed therefore unto yourselves, and to all the
flock, over the which the Holy Ghost hath made you
overseers, to feed the church of God, which he hath
purchased with his own blood.*

*For I know this, that after my departing
shall grievous wolves enter in among you,
not sparing the flock.*

*Also of your own selves shall men arise
speaking perverse things,
to draw away disciples after them.*

*Therefore watch, and remember, that by
the space of three years I ceased not to warn*

every one night and day with tears.

ACTS 20:27-31

FOOTNOTES

[1] *The Passion: Photography from the Movie* The Passion of the Christ, (Icon Distribution, Tyndale 2004) from the foreword.

[2] Mel Gibson, interview by Raymond Arroyo, *The World Over Live*, EWTN, January 13, 2004.

[3] Ibid.

[4] Medved, Michael, "Gibson's right to his 'Passion,'" *The Christian Science Monitor* February 2, 2004.

[5] Gibson/Arroyo interview.

[6] *The Canons and Degrees of the Council of Trent*, ed. and trans. H.J. Schroeder, O.P. (Tan Books, 1978) Sixth Session, Can. 30, 46.

[7] Second Vatican Council, "Dogmatic Constitution on Divine Revelation," no. 9.

[8] Neff, David, "The Passion of Mel Gibson," *Christianity Today*, March 2004, 30,32.

[9] Neff, *Christianity Today*, 32.

[10] Emmerich, Anne Catherine, *The Dolorous Passion of Our Lord Jesus Christ*, (Rockford, IL: TAN Books and Publishers, 1983) 136.

[11] Emmerich, *Dolorous*, 149-150.

[12] Sister Mary of Jesus, *The Mystical City of God*, (New Jersey: Ave Maria Institute, 1949) Volume III, 652.

[13] Gibson/Arroyo interview.

[14] Gibson/Arroyo interview.

[15] Ryan, Tim, "Embodying Christ," *Honolulu Star Bulletin*, February 22, 2004, http://www.firstthings.com/ftissues/ft9405/mission.html.

[16] Ryan, *Honolulu Star Bulletin.*

[17] Email on file with the author.

[18] Allen, John L., Jr. "The Word From Rome," *National Catholic Reporter*, vol, 3, no. 30, March 19, 2004, http://www.nationalcatholicreporter.org/word/pfw031904.htm.

[19] Allen, *National Catholic Reporter.*

[20] Henry, Matthew, *Matthew Henry's Commentary on the Whole Bible* (Hendrickson Publishers, 1994), on Isaiah 52:3.

[21] Hunt, Dave, "God is Love," *The Berean Call,* April 2004.

[22] Email on file with the author.

[23] The Medjugorje website: medjugorje.hr/int%20Caviezel%20ENG.htm.

[24] Neff, *Christianity Today,* March 2004, 30.

[25] Neff, *Christianity Today,* March 2004, 34.

[26] *L.A. Times,* December 25, 1998.

[27] Stanford, Ray, *Fatima Prophecy* (Ballantine Books, 1988).

[28] Schleifer, Aliah, *Mary the Blessed Virgin of Islam* (Aliah Schleifer, 1997), 64.

[29] Beyer, Richard, *Medjugorje Day By Day (*Ave Maria Press, 1993).

[30] Madrid, Patrick, *Surprised By Truth* (Bascilica Press, 1994), 239-240.

[31] http://kutai.kinabalu.net/ scotthahn.html#journey.

[32] Neff, *Christianity Today,* 34.

[33] *Our Lady of Fatima's Peace Plan from Heaven* (Tan Books and Publishers, 1983), inside back cover.

[34] Neff, *Christianity Today* 34.

[35] Honeycutt, Kirk, "The Passion of the Christ," *The Hollywood Reporter,* February 23, 2004, http://www.hollywoodreporter.com/thr/reviews/review_display.jsp?vnu_content_id=1000441264.

[36] Ebert, Roger, "Gibson's 'Passion' Graphically shows the horrific price Jesus paid," *The Bend Bulletin,* section B, February 25, 2004.

[37] Ebert, *The Bend Bulletin.*

[38] Gibson/Arroyo interview.

[39] Neff, *Christianity Today,* 35.

[40] Neff, *Christianity Today,* 34.

[41] Hutchinson, Robert J., "A Passionate Response to Mel Gibson's Film," *Inside the Vatican,* March/April 2004, 24.

[42] Ebert, *The Bend Bulletin.*

[43] *The Catholic Encyclopedia* Online Edition, 2003, http://www.newadvent.org/cathen/15569a.htm.

[44] *Redemptoris Mater,* "On the Blessed Virgin Mary in the Life of the Pilgrim Church," Encyclical of Pope John Paul II, March 25, 1987.

[45] Miravalle, Dr. Mark, "Gibson's Passion and Mary 'Co-Redemptrix,'" *Inside the Vatican,* March-April 2004, 20.

[46] See author's article on the subject, "Mormon Fiction," August 2003 <thebereancall.org>.

[47] *Unitatis Redintegration,* Chapter I, Catholic Principles on Ecumenism.

[48] *Unitatis Redintegration,* Chapter II, Catholic Principles on Ecumenism.

[49] See author's article on the subject, "*Com*promise Keepers," November 1995, <thebereancall.org>.

[50] Editors of Catholic Exchange, *A Guide to the Passion,* (Westchester, PA: Ascension Press, 2004), 2.

[51] *Catechism of the Catholic Church,* (New York: William Sadler, Inc., 1994), paragraph 1374.

[52] Ibid., paragraph 1366.

[53] Ibid., paragraph 1392.

[54] Second Vatican Council, "Sacred Liturgy," "Instruction on the Worship of the Eucharistic Mystery," no. 7.

[55] Gibson/Arroyo interview.

[56] Second Vatican Council, "Sacred Liturgy," "Instruction on the Worship of the Eucharistic Mystery," no. 3b.

[57] *The Passion: Photography from the Movie*, foreword.

[58] Neff, *CT*, 35.

[59] Armstrong, Chris, "The Fountain Fill'd with Blood," *Christianity Today*, March 2004, 44.

[60] http://www.youthspecialties.com/free/programming/stations.

[61] Tozer, A.W., *Tozer on Worship and Entertainment,* compiled by James L. Snyder, (Camp Hill, PA: Christian Publications, Inc., 1997), 183-84.

[62] Ibid., 189–190.

[63] Ibid., 192.

[64] Ibid., 192–193.

[65] Ibid., 195.

[66] Ibid., 197.

[67] Ibid., 197.

[68] Ibid., 199.

[69] Ibid., 202.

[70] Ibid., 204–205.

[71] Ibid., 208.

[72] Ibid., 208–209.

[73] Hunt, Dave, *A Woman Rides the Beast* (Harvest House Publishers, 1994), 44-45.

ABOUT THE BEREAN CALL

The Berean Call (TBC) is a nonprofit,
tax-exempt corporation which exists to:

ALERT believers in Christ to unbiblical teachings and practices
impacting the church

EXHORT believers to give greater heed to biblical discernment
and truth regarding teachings and practices being
currently promoted in the church

SUPPLY believers with teaching, information, and materials
which will encourage the love of God's truth, and assist in
the development of biblical discernment

MOBILIZE believers in Christ to action in obedience to the
scriptural command to "earnestly contend for the faith"
(Jude 3)

IMPACT the church of Jesus Christ with the necessity for
trusting the Scriptures as the only rule for faith, practice,
and a life pleasing to God

A free monthly newsletter, THE BEREAN CALL, *may be received by sending*
a request to: PO Box 7019, Bend, OR 97708; or by calling 1-800-937-6638.

To register for free e-mail updates, to access our digital archives, and to
order a variety of additional resource materials online, visit us at:

www.thebereancall.org